S.W.A.G.

THE LONG WALK IN MY SHOES

Written by Glen Norman

AuthorHouse™
1663 Liberty Drive
Bloomington, IN 47403
www.authorhouse.com
Phone: 1 (800) 839-8640

Published by AuthorHouse 01/23/2015

ISBN: 978-1-4969-6274-4 (sc)
ISBN: 978-1-4969-6275-1 (e)

Any people depicted in stock imagery provided by Thinkstock are models,
and such images are being used for illustrative purposes only.
Certain stock imagery © Thinkstock.

This book is printed on acid-free paper.

Because of the dynamic nature of the Internet, any web addresses or links contained in this book may have changed
since publication and may no longer be valid. The views expressed in this work are solely those of the author and do not
necessarily reflect the views of the publisher, and the publisher hereby disclaims any responsibility for them.

Everybody has a devastating story to tell;

even though I'm just another person,

God told me to share mine so that's what I'll do,

whether it touches your heart or not

What is pain, hardship, failure, success, criticism, fear, hatred, love, peace, crime, death, or life? No one ever opens their eyes for the first time expecting to experience any of these things. As we grow everyday under the care of the people we came to know as our parents, all we tend to receive is nurture, love, and happiness. When negative situations arise in our lives, we tend to ask the most feared question…why? At a young age we are told that there is a God to believe in who will protect us from evil, but disputations form when evil still happens even after we pray for God's protection. Over time, we come to find out that there is no answer to these types of questions and only with true living faith can you attain security in your beliefs. As a young man, I lost all faith in God because I believed he failed to respond in my most dire time of need. After losing my faith, my mindset was to live on pure luck and anything good that happened to me would only be considered luck. I constantly questioned God for answers regarding my purpose in life because I had no idea which route to take. Walk with me as I take you on the journey of my life. Put on my shoes without actually wearing them and see where I lead you. This is my story…

In memory of

Angela Denise Briggs

Glen Paul Norman Sr.

Glennisha Briggs I

And also for my siblings:

Glennisha Briggs II

Rochelle Briggs Brailey

Kendrick Briggs

Brandon Norman

Cleandre Norman

CONTENTS

CHAPTER 1:

My childhood was ordinary in the sense that I lived a normal life growing up, at least that's what I thought. I lived with my mom, Angela, my younger sister, Glennisha, and my older sister, Rochelle. We lived in the small town of Abbeville, Louisiana that carried a capacity of roughly three thousand people. It was just the three of us for the most part, but when I was four my mom married a man I thought was weird. My three older brothers lived in separate parts of the world. Brandon and, Cleandre, lived somewhere in California and my other brother, Kendrick, was locked away in a prison somewhere in Virginia. We had one other sister who had a congenital condition that caused her to die at birth.

Life for us was unstable at times because the relationship between my mom and her husband was tense at times and she would always go from job to job forcing us to move to different homes but still remaining in the same city. We started living in Live Oak Manor, also known as the projects, then we moved to some apartments on East Street near my grandma, then to a small yellow house, then to a white house on Lafayette Street, until finally moving with my mom's husband to a mobile home just down the road from the white house. All of these moves happened up until I was ten, but after that we decided to settle in to the mobile home.

It was 2001 when we moved into the mobile home, the same year two commercial airplanes crashed into the World Trade Center. That incident struck fear across the nation as it put our country into a war overseas. I didn't think too much of it at the time because I was at the powerless age of ten and there was not much I could do about anything but just hope things would get better. I can remember my cousin, Jamal, and his group making a song about the tragedy and that I thought was good enough to go viral. The new mobile home allowed me to have some privacy with my own room. So on days I didn't want to be bothered I would just hide away in my room and watch movies about the military. Every morning before school my mom had us clean our rooms, wash dishes, and vacuum. Since I was the only boy in the house, besides my mom's husband, I had to do the dishes a lot. Growing up with only girls was hard because they always got their way with things making me do the chores they hated doing. My older sister made me do all her chores because she was pregnant for her first baby at the time. I would get upset and lie on the couch fussing at her for delegating duties and not wanting to help. Instead of her fussing back she would ignore me until I really got underneath her skin causing her to swing at me. I was lying down when she did so my first reaction was to kick back and I accidentally kicked her in the stomach. Fear struck my heart because I didn't want to hurt her baby: my future niece.

Many times I went into thinking (I was always thinking about something as a kid) and asking myself a multitude of questions as if I were having a conversation with someone of a high intellectual level who can actually answer them. My mind rambled off with questions such as: Where is my dad? Is the world coming to an end (watching too much zombie movies? I guess)? Will I see past age ten? Will I ever have a little brother that will look up to me? When can I meet my older brothers? Etcetera… Just some questions that I hoped can be answered thoroughly one day. My mom always caught me in my deep dazes and had to snap her fingers in front of my face to get my attention. She would tell me all the time that I think about things way too much and I should relax more.

I asked my mom when would I get to talk to my dad, or see him, since all I really knew was my stepdad, which I hated because we didn't get a long. I was eager to know who my actual dad was, and if he existed I wanted to know where have he been my whole life. She sat me down saying, "Son you do have a dad but he lives in California at the moment and we are not on good terms but if he call I'll let you speak to him." I patiently waited for days to hear from him but never got the call I so desperately wanted. I spent ten years without him already, so my thoughts led me to believe that he didn't really care about his own son.

Some time after my eleventh birthday in 2002, I got a call from my dad wishing me happy birthday and apologizing for being to busy to call me like he wanted to. His way of wanting to make up to me was offering me a chance to go visit him in California during the summer. Although, I viewed him more as a stranger than a dad, I still wanted to take this opportunity to know him better. Trying to convince my mom was my next task but she finally agreed to let me go for a couple weeks during the summer time.

When the day finally came for him to come pick me up, I started getting nervous wondering how an actual face-to-face conversation with him would be. It felt awkward meeting a man claiming to be my dad for the first time, but I was ready for him to take to me California so I didn't let that thought bother me. Looking at him in person put me under the impression that he took real good care of himself just like I did because we were both on the chubby side, except he was much more taller and had bigger shoulders than I. His head and face were both big and round, just like mine. It was scary seeing a man that looked very similar to me, or better yet, me looking like a splitting image of him. Not only did we carry the same characteristics physically, but we also acted the same way mentally, which was weird to see.

Being in so much of a rush, I started forgetting things that I needed the most. Luckily, my mom was right there behind me making sure I didn't forget anything. After I finished packing, I kissed my mom bye while watching the hurt harbor her eyes from me leaving her grasp. Around this time, she was in and out of the hospital for her lungs collapsing frequently so that was my main worry about leaving her for two weeks. Considering the fact that, I was too young to really help out in any way I just felt that she would need me if something were to happen.

When we landed in California, I stretched out inhaling a deep breath of fresh California air getting ready to enjoy my vacation in the big city. I always heard about California in my Geography class and wanted to visit so I was really enjoying this. Being so amazed with how beautiful the scenery was, my dad would try to get my attention but had to say my name multiple times then tap my arm because I was so drawn in to the big buildings and mountains that was far off in the distance but big enough to seem as if they were closer. On the bus, leaving the airport headed to where my dad were living, he would point out places that he wanted to take me. I just agreed to everything because I didn't care what we did I was just happy to finally be with him for the first time. I couldn't believe that I was actually about to be roaming around California! When we made it to Fairfield the first place he took me was to see my aunt, Jani, her husband, Karl, my brother, Brandon, my cousins, and other family that I didn't know I had. They were happy to see me for the first time because before then they had just heard a lot about me.

My dad and I spent a lot of time with them throughout my visit. They took me all over California from places like; Water world, Marine world, six flags, fishing, and some place where you could play laser tag. The two weeks seemed like it flew by because we were always out doing something fun. Them and my dad left a really good impression on me so I knew that this would definitely be a place I want to come to again if I ever get another chance.

Even though I spent majority of my life without my dad being there for me, this little time we shared together made it seem as if we didn't miss a day. In this brief period, I learned more about his personality and what he loves to do, realizing that we had a ton of things in common made me appreciate him for coming back for me. I tied in pretty much every emotion possible before I left because I enjoyed the fact that we created such a close bond despite all the time we spent separated. Before meeting him, I always dreamed that this day would come and when it came to an end it hurt me very deeply. As he let go of my hand in the airport, my eyes immediately began to water as if it would be the last time I get to see him.

Returning back home, I still spent a great deal of time trying to establish a bond with my mom husband but we never really connected on a lot of things. I tried to treat him like he was my biological father because I was desperate to have that male role model all the time, but no matter how hard I tried he always found ways to make me want to disconnect from him. Some days I wouldn't have to deal with him because my mom would kick him out after they argued for hours. Seeing my mom stress wasn't a good sight for me knowing she was sick most of the time and I didn't know how to help her.

If I wasn't at school, with my friends or messing with my sister, I spent all my time glued to my mom since she stayed stressed and I didn't have a male figure to look up too. My mom was always the sweetest when it came to nurturing me in my time of need. I loved wrapping myself in her arms as she rocked me to sleep and kissed my forehead reassuring my safety is in her hands. Besides the love and nurture she shared with us, there were also times when she would get mad at us. The belt, along with many other things that was within her reach became something she used to discipline us. Even though I hated when she whipped us it never stopped me from loving her unconditionally. It made me realize that there are consequences for every action and she made sure we learned that very early on.

We started noticing more that my mom condition was getting worse and she was losing strength by not being able to do as much as she used too. We tried not to think much of it since our assumptions led us to believe that it was because of work and that she was just too tired to really do anything. Most of the time, when my sisters would leave to go spend a night at our other family house I would stay home to make sure she was all right. Even though she loved the fact that I wanted to stay, she would always force me to go hang out with other family and friends. I refused consistently but ultimately she made me leave while she stayed home alone since her husband worked offshore. Being away from her during those times were hard so I would call repeatedly in the middle of the night to check on her. It was very seldom that she would need to go to the hospital but when she did it made me fear that the conditions were worst than originally expected. The doctors did many full body tests on her only to find nothing was wrong, which left me in a sigh of relief. Even though they didn't find anything I stayed worried because I felt as if they were lying.

Suddenly, she began showing signs of strength again as she was able to go back to work and still have the ability to have fun with us after she got off. It made me feel good to watch her back at full strength because seeing her sick was unusual to me. I always thought of her as the queen; the one that never gets hurt and can stand strong against anything. When I felt assured that she was going to be okay, I went enjoy some outside time with my friends from school and my little sister. I tried to make the most of my childhood moments even though the thought of my mom getting sick at any moment constantly ran through my mind.

In the early part of 2003, just turning twelve, I felt like a man almost immediately after my birthday especially since I had hormonal explosions going through every inch of my body. I started flirting with girls more; well at least I can say I was just braver to walk up to them even though rejection happened sometimes. I asked my mom when would I get to talk to my dad again because I wanted to hopefully get some advice on how to talk to girls but that never happened. I heard many stories about how my dad from some of my family how he used to get beat up by my uncles all the time and how he never stayed faithful to any woman he talked to, so I just erased the thought about asking him anything. My mom never got back to me on talking to him again so I gave up thinking about trying anymore.

As the summer began approaching, we begged our mom to get us that big swimming pool we saw at Wal-Mart every time we went grocery shopping because it would be too hot to do anything else. We made sure we found our way to the pool section staying there until our mom found us so she would have no choice but to see the pool we wanted. I looked forward to the summer especially since the two years I spent in the fifth grade for misconduct set me back a bit. I knew that when the new school year began I would be able to finally walk amongst the bigger kids in middle school when the new school year started would feel like a huge accomplishment.

When the school year came to an end that had to be the best bus ride I had all year long. My mom had already finished her favorite dessert, which was her special pecan candy that I got to help prepare the night before! I loved helping her stir the pecan candy because I always got to lick the spoon after. As the bus pulled up to my trailer, I hesitated a bit to get off because in the front yard was a pool already filled with water just waiting on me to get in it! I almost thought it wouldn't my house so I stayed on the bus for a second looking around to verify that it was, but my sister said, "Come on, dude, let's go call everybody so we could all swim." I was still in shock, with excitement over the roof as I slowly walked off the bus. I ran into the house and gave my mom the biggest hug and kiss ever. "Can we go swimming momma, I said." She looked at me and said, "Well I didn't buy this big pool for nobody to get in it."

We invited some of our cousins and family to come swim and eat pecan with us. Literally every kid in our family started showing up at our trailer. Before you know it we had our first swimming party without even realizing it. While we were swimming, I remember my sister asking our cousin to grab her Snicker since he was already running in the house to grab something to eat too. When he came back to the door with the Snicker my sister yells, "Throw it! I'll catch it!" So he threw it but as she went to catch it the water on her hands allowed the Snicker to slip through her fingertips knocking her right in the mouth making her bite a hole in her lip. My sister ran into the house crying like she was about to die. It wouldn't funny when it happened but later that night when mom held another card game all the kids stayed out to play and we made fun of.

Every time my mom had a card game it was like our cue to have fun without adults interrupting us. We would ride our bikes up and down the street racing to see who had the fastest bike. My cousin, Cliff, asked me to race him passed the corner store; little did I know my life would flash right before my eyes because as we were in full speed my handle bars fell forward completely forcing me to lose control of the bike running right into a parked car on the right side of the road. When I hit the car, the left handle bar passed near my left eye missing it by only a half an inch. After that incident, that was the last time I rode a bike for a few months because I was scared of it happening again and not being lucky to survive it next time. That continued to be my phobia even after I became brave enough to ride a bike again.

Not to long after my incident, I heard from my dad again when he called for a few minutes checking to see how everything was going with my sister and I. Since I had the chance to spend time with him previously, it made me wonder why him and my mom wasn't together. As a kid, I couldn't pass judgment on something I didn't really understand but it was always a thought in the back of mind. He would speak very highly of my mom to me saying that she is a great woman and how much he cares about her. Seemed to me that he was worth another chance with her but once again it was not my place to be considering that since I was only a kid. My mom always stressed to me that kids have to stay out of grown folks business anyway. I tried talking to my mom about it sometimes but she would always try to avoid the conversation.

As the summer came to an end, the first day of school was right around the corner so we had to go do a lot of shopping for our school clothes and supplies. We had to wear uniforms that consisted of brown Dickie style shorts or pants and our shirts had to be white, black, or red so it was not hard to shop for clothes. The only thing that made you standout was your haircut and the shoes you wore. The first day of school was always your best shot at making that good first impression on someone.

The only thing I was worried about beginning the sixth grade was how hard the classes would be. I knew that as I went up in school it would get more challenging, so I had to mentally prepare myself for what I was about to be getting into. I feared that since the fifth grade gave me struggles then the sixth grade wouldn't be any easier. I was also happy that I would finally be able to be with all my friends again. I wouldn't planning on being the class clown this time since I was focused on catching up with the others that left me behind and I was tired of getting whipped with the belt or anything my mom used that was within arms reach of her.

We started school on August 15th, 2003, which was a Friday so it was a breeze to get through class knowing that the weekend was about to start again. My weekend didn't go so good though because my mom had another collapsed lung attack and was sent back into intensive care. I mainly spent my whole weekend by her bedside making sure she knew that I was gone be there to support her. The feeling of not being able to fix her wounds didn't stop me from being by her side. It hurt me to see her lying in the hospital bed again because in my mind I always pictured her as the Queen Bee (Strongest woman there ever was) so it really took me by surprise watching her lie there helpless.

My family told me to just pray about it but as a kid I didn't think praying would help this type of situation. I always trusted in the doctors keeping faith in them believing that they will cure her and have her back up and running like nothing ever happened. I can remember looking my mom in the eyes and holding her hand while she lied there telling me how much she loves me. Leaving her bedside was hard for me; as I walked away I told her I'd be back after classes were over. I got to my first class, which was math and while the teacher started going over the first lesson the intercom came on with the principal calling me to the front office. In shock, I rose from my seat wondering if I did anything wrong. As I approached the office, I saw my Aunt sitting there with my sister waiting for me. The principal told me I was dismissed from class for the day and me not thinking anything wrong with that, I automatically felt excitement to be leaving school and not be in any trouble.

Meanwhile my brother, who was released from prison a while back, stayed right next to her that Sunday night. The next morning he woke up and noticed her not responding to anything. When he realized this he ran out the room yelling for the nurses come check on her. Doctors and nurses came running trying to revive her, doing so for about ten minutes but didn't see any success. After repeatedly trying, they stopped all operations and pronounced her dead at 12:42 that afternoon. While all this was going on, I was still getting ready to leave school after being dismissed.

For some reason, I had a gut feeling that something was wrong because although my Aunt wouldn't crying then I can still see the sadness on her face as if something terrible had happened. I didn't start to get worried until we pulled up to the hospital. As I was going up the elevator to where my mom was, I immediately started to feel pain inside like a professional boxer was punching me in my stomach repeatedly. I got off the elevator and slowly walked to her room while preparing myself for the worse but still hoping for the best. When I finally got to the door of her room, I saw her lying there with her eyes bulging as if they were about to burst out of her eye sockets…she was dead. I stood there in shock crying out loud and not moving towards her because I was too scared and it was the first time for me seeing something like this. I couldn't believe she was lying there dead right there in front of me. I can remember my older sister telling me to go kiss her and say my last goodbyes but I didn't want to move because it was all too real for me to bear. I finally felt some strength to walk towards her slowly but I never actually touched or kissed her I just walked away crying even harder than before. I still regret that I didn't give her a last kiss to this day.

My brother went on a rampage while my family and I was in the room crying ours out. It was hard for the nurses to calm him down so they had to call the police on him especially when he punched a hole in the wall the size of a grapefruit. I thought he was going to go to jail again but the police understood the situation so they grabbed him and walked him out of the hospital. They covered my mom body with a sheet as my family started to walk out the hospital. That had to be the worst feeling seeing my mom being covered and carried away. Strange thoughts of me hurting myself and joining my mom in Heaven crossed my mind. Suicide seemed like it was going to be the best option at the time.

Being twelve years old, I worried that all my support, love, care, and nurture was all gone. The intense emotions of feeling lost, lonely, and hurt covered my heart and my next steps in life seemed as if it would come to an end before it even started. My sister and I were crushed completely because having her around on a daily basis was something we were so used to that it hurt just that much more knowing that she would not be there no more. I held my sister tight letting her know that I will be there for her through this but I wasn't sure how strong I could actually be. I didn't even know if I could even take care of myself much less help her get through this pain as well.

Walking in our trailer after the fact to clear it out brought back many flashbacks that was just to unbearable for me so I let everyone else go through her things. Although, I missed out on grabbing some things that I could take with me and hold close to my heart as sentimental value, I trusted that my other family would give it to me later. Everything was happening so fast that it felt as if it were a dream. Throughout the day, I would occasionally pinch myself hoping that it would help me wake up but when bedtime rolled around my hope slowly died.

On the day of the funeral, my cousin, Jamal, and I did a song in front of the church called 'God send me and Angel'. It was hard for me to really do the song since all I wanted to do was cry while watching her body lie there in front of me. The whole time I was just wishing that she would just wake up from a deep sleep but it never happened. When we left the church to go bury her, I cried heavily because the hope for her to just wake up and have everything go back to normal was slowly fading. As they laid her to rest I turned my head not wanting to see her go in the ground. Leaving the graveyard, I looked back while wiping my old tears away trying to keep up with the new tears that followed.

I was still lost in a daze still hoping that this would be a dream and that I will eventually wake up and again everything would be back to normal. The ride back home was so quiet, all I can think about was, Why her? Why? My mom is too strong. When I got back to the trailer, my family had already cleared her place getting all the valuables that my mom left behind. It upset me because it seemed as if they couldn't wait to take all her stuff from the trailer leaving me with really nothing too take for myself. I at least wanted something that I can hold at night so that I can still feel like she was right there with me. Being twelve years old, I didn't really understand what was going on so the thought of suicide stayed there but fear kept that thought from being put into action.

The next day we had a barbecue outside the trailer in honor of my mom death. At the time I really didn't understand why we were having what seemed to be a party because I felt that it was not a time for celebration. I remember asking my grandma why we were partying and she said, "It's not a party baby, it's just a tradition to honor your mom death because you are supposed to be happy that she is going to be living with God." I didn't get it at the time but I knew she meant good by it since it was her daughter so I knew she was hurting inside still.

One day, my sister and I were sitting outside by the projects, where one of my cousins lived, just crying, and not really talking much. We both were left clueless as to what would happen for us next. That day we got a call from my dad in California saying he heard the bad news and he will be on his way down to come pick us up as soon as he can. Still feeling a lot of pain inside, I remembered my previous visit out there and knew in my mind that it would be all right to go out there and live with him. About a week later he showed up and my family didn't want him to take us all the way across the world with him since they didn't believe he would take care of us. They even called the police to try and stop him from taking us, but the cops said there was no reason for them to stop him so they couldn't intervene. Leaving all my family hurt me the most because I didn't know when I would be able to see all of them again. It also hurt me inside to leave the place that I was familiar with and all my friends but for some reason I felt it would be a good change for me…for us.

Chapter 2:

When we landed at the airport the place seemed different this time. I didn't get the same vibe I had when I visited the first time. "Where are we? I asked." He looked at me and said, "East Oakland, California, this is where I live now." I didn't think much of it at the time because I thought maybe this bad feeling would eventually go away. Maybe it was thought of me knowing that I just lost my mom. Walking around the airport trying to leave was almost impossible since it was so crowded. I nearly bumped into everyone and my rolling bag that trailed behind me rolled over most people feet. Finally, we made it to the bus that took us right into the neighborhood where my dad lived.

The bus dropped us off at the corner store down the road so we had to walk a good distance to get to his apartment. On my right was a Chevron gas station filled with a bunch a gangsters loitering around the building like they owned the lot or something, and on my left was an abandoned building which seemed to be where all the gangsters lived. As we kept walking, I noticed the neighborhood looked beat down and ghetto like this area attracted all types of trouble. I said a small prayer in my head hoping that nothing bad would happen, even though I didn't know that my prayer would actually be heard I did it anyway.

The very next week my dad took both my sister and I to register for school. At this time, I was just beginning the sixth grade so I was kind of nervous going to school amongst the bigger kids and not knowing any of them. The thought of just losing my mom also took my sense of protection away. Taking on a new school with new people in a new environment with out my mom took a lot of courage and bravery. I went to class that same day while my dad took my sister to the elementary school since she was starting the fourth grade that year. She didn't like the fact that we had to go to separate schools but when she started making some friends the separation between us became a little easier for her. Since school wasn't too far from where we lived, every morning my sister and I would walk to school. Surprisingly, walking the dangerous streets of East Oakland we made it too and from school everyday by ourselves. My dad never wanted to walk with us, which I thought to be very unmanly of him. The only time he would get up is just to make sure we were getting ready for school and then he would go back to bed.

The only time I faced a scare is when I walked home by myself one day and a man came out of nowhere pointing a gun to my face saying, "WHAT YOU HAVE LIL NIGGA!" I just stood there in shock digging in my pockets handing him the few dollars I had so that he could leave me alone. He stood there for a moment as if he was thinking about shooting me but the car that was about to pass frightened him away. For a few minutes or so, I stood there replaying what just happened to me because everything went so fast. I wasn't far from home but a few seconds later, the vehicle coming down the road was my dad, who pulled up in his motor home to pick me up and had my sister riding with him. I never told them what happened because he wasn't going to do anything about it anyway.

School for me wasn't so fun because the older kids had already developed what we like to call style or swag and that was something I didn't have. I wore Shaquille O'Neal shoes from payless that my dad bought for me, and my outfit looked as if I were still living in the 70s and 80s because I would wear my dad old button down Hawaiian looking shirts that got me teased on a daily basis. It took me awhile to even make a few friends but I usually tried to stay to myself. I really didn't know how to protect myself at the time and I knew my dad wasn't going to protect me neither.

My sister met a friend named, Ash, who she spent a lot of time with throughout the school semester. I would go over there every once in awhile just so I can be around her friend because I had a crush on her. Every time we went visit, my sister would make every attempt to leave us in the room together so that I could have the chance to talk to her alone but I would always be too nervous to do that so I would write her sweet letters instead. Ash, told me I had a bit of cockiness I never seemed to think so.

My sister stayed in the house watching Disney Channel most of the time. I had my Xbox that I could play but I couldn't play that much since my sister didn't want to miss her shows. We argued all the time about who get to use the TV next and of course she would get the benefit of the doubt.

One day while I was sitting outside on the steps some guys from across the street walks up to me, asking where was I from; I guess since they never saw me in this area before. "What's your name homie don't sound like from around here?" He said. I told him "My name is Glen, I'm from Abbeville, Louisiana." After I said that he had a confused look on his face as if he ate something sour then he turned and said, "From where! Abdumville?" I just shook my head and said "no, Abbeville." I still don't think he fully understood what I said so he just ignored it and asked me to come hang out with them at his place across the street. At the time, I think my dad was in the house sleeping or something so I told him I'll go, I just can't stay long because I don't want my dad to come outside and see me gone. "Its cool man I understand…now come on," He said. I got up from my seat looked back for a quick second then followed him and his friends to their place. It was just myself, two others, and him playing madden on the Xbox.

I sat there for a while watching them play just talking and getting to know all the guys. They were questioning me like I was in the middle of a big interview making me nervous. After the game was over we went out the backyard and played basketball for a while. Everything was going good until the mood changed with one of the guys while we were shooting around. He asked me if I ever been apart of a gang or anything. I shook my head in response without saying a word. Then he pushed me asking if I wanted to be apart of their "click". In my mind, I wanted to say no because I was a terrified that it would only lead me into doing things that would cause nothing but trouble. I agreed anyway because I didn't want them thinking that I was punking out. Right after I said that they immediately started jumping me, so all I could do is fight back the best I could. After about five minutes of being brutally beaten, they picked me up and dusted me off.

"That was considered your initiation into our gang lil bruh… we don't wear certain colors cuz we don't wanna stand out, so we just keep it on the low you feel me," one of the guys said. I just nodded saying, "Ok cool, I got you." Fear remained in my heart, but I knew I had to toughen up if I wanted to survive being around these guys.

The walk home was painful but I tried like I was all right so it can look like nothing happened. My legs and arms were scratched up from them hitting me on a big cement block when I fell. My dad asked me what happened but I never told him anything, I just said I was playing on the stairs and fell. I never even told my sister what happened just in case my dad would ask her and I didn't want to worry about it slipping out of her mouth.

The gang I became a part of were into a lot of bad things like robbing the corner store, fighting, breaking into people houses taking most of their valuables, and selling drugs. I remember one day they forced me to go steal from the store right down the street from my apartment. It wasn't hard, but my heart was pounding like bass coming from a fifteen-inch subwoofer. Besides, this was the first time I ever did anything to that extent before. I grabbed all the stuff they wanted and took off running as fast as I could out the store. The guy behind the counter saw me running but I was out so fast that all I heard him say was, "HEY KID!" Before I zoomed out the door. I was scared to go back thinking that the guy may have saw my face and would call the cops next time he saw me. Eventually, I had no choice but to go since my dad always sent us there to get something to eat when there was no food in the house. Thankfully the guy didn't really catch my face on the way out. In the inside I can feel the guilt of doing what I did, but I had to play that off when I was around them so they could believe I didn't care.

Another day, when we were all just sitting at his house playing the game one of the guys jumped up saying, "Man remember ole boy that say he not scared to take us on? Let's go get that fool man I think he home." All four of us went over to his house but when we got close enough to see who was in the house we hid in the bushes waiting for the perfect opportunity to bust in. One dude stood outside smoking a cigarette so we waited until he was done before we made our move. As soon as he started walking in, we came running behind him. I kicked the guy in the back, which made him fly unto the floor, and then I punched the dude in the face that was sitting on the couch playing the game. In the midst of this, his mom was in the kitchen hearing what was going on she started screaming while reaching for her phone to call the police. One of my gang members grabbed the Xbox and smashed it on the ground, and then we just ran out.

That week when I went back to school some tall black dude approached me in class and said we have business to handle. In my mind I'm thinking he found out about what happened and that must have been his brother or something. Since I had nobody from my gang there to back me up I was nervous when the bell ring for us to switch classes. It didn't help that you had to walk outside to get to every class. When the bell rang he came up to me fussing saying, "was that yo lil click that ran in on my lil brother the other day?" I stood there nervously saying, "man I don't know what you talking about." He just stopped talking and pushed me to the ground; as I got back up he punched me in the face dropping me again. This time I didn't get up, the principal came and broke up the fight bringing us both to the office. He suspended me for three days but left the other dude alone and told me to be careful with the guys in the school, I think he was scared too…honestly. It seemed as if the principal and the teachers were being recruited into these gangs.

Hanging around with the gang opened my eyes to a different type of lifestyle that I wasn't accustomed too. I started learning more about different type of drugs, pills and alcohol. I tried to avoid doing drugs or smoking mainly because I made an oath to myself so that I can avoid getting lung cancer like my mom. Even though I made an oath, they forced me to smoke weed and every time I took a puff I coughed hard enough to the point that it felt like my lungs were getting ready to explode out of my chest. The thought of my mom dealing with lung cancer worried me and had me thinking that just one puff would kill me. They would all pass the blunt around multiple times and had one rolled waiting to be put into rotation. In the meantime, I sat there watching them all pass out on the couch from getting too high.

Being a disorganized small town gang we didn't carry guns. Most of the other gangs that surrounded the area did carry weapons but if we ever confronted any of them we always handled problems by fighting. We gained respect around the hood just by our method of handling situations. Selling drugs was another way we gained respect but I was never apart of that, I would be around sometimes when the transactions were taken place. It was crazy how we were all young teens dealing with adults that came to my gang for drugs.

I never bothered to wake him up and let him know I made it back from school because I was scared he would snap, so I went to my room and watched Disney channel with my sister until he woke up.

One night he came home intoxicated, and bust in our room complaining about the house not being clean. He grabbed us both and started beating us until scars, welts and blood showed. He even threw our TV and my Xbox against the wall shattering it into pieces. I can even see the fear in his girlfriend face. Not long after, I heard sirens outside as if the cops were heading to our house, I guess the neighbors heard the racquet and called the police. When I peaked out my window, the cops, the child protective service, the ambulance, the fire department, and even some neighbors were outside watching. I was surprised we didn't end up on the news with the scene we were making. The cops questioned my dad but of course he came up with an alibi to avoid getting arrested. Some of the agents questioned us but, out of fear, but we had to lie.

Eventually, he was busted with possession of drugs and somehow bribed his way out of a jail sentence as well. He was always good at manipulating others in believing anything he wanted them too. While he was locked up we used that time to sneak and use the phone to call back home for help. Our cousin, Teedy, was one of the first people we were able to contact. We told her to come get us because we feared for our lives. She gave us support through the phone but I don't think she had the ability to really come get us at the time. At that point, we tried to hang in there hoping that one day we could go back home to our family. Once again, the thoughts of suicide crossed my mind, but there was always a voice in my head telling me to keep trying. I believed it was my mom or God but I had no idea exactly but I still listened. I also didn't want to leave my little sister alone and I know she needed me to be her role model.

About two weeks before Christmas my dad finally got released from jail and immediately made us pack our things. He was in the worst attitude griping about everything that happened before he went to jail. In our mind we were going back home to Louisiana but I had a feeling that we weren't. Even though we had mostly everything packed we stayed and spent Christmas there before we left.

It was our first Christmas with him and it turned out to be a complete nightmare. I always wanted another remote control car, some video games, and a bike. I can't quite remember exactly what my sister wanted that year but I'm pretty sure one of the items on her list was bike too. She always seemed too want the same of things I wanted. On Christmas Eve, my dad put a couple boxes of Christmas cookies underneath the little three-foot tall tree he got from the dollar store. Our holiday spirit disappeared as we both accepted the fact that we were really not going to have a good Christmas this year. My dad tried telling us that Santa is bringing our gifts in the morning hoping that would make us feel better, but we already lost hope so it didn't make a difference no matter what he said.

When the morning came, we jumped out of bed and ran into the living room hoping to start opening gifts but there was nothing but the same box of cookies from the night before. It hurt our hearts especially since he didn't even get out of bed until eleven o' clock that day, so it seemed as if he didn't care. When he finally woke up he walked in our room told us Merry Christmas and told us to come sit in the living room with him. He said, "I apologize my babies I just can't afford any gifts this year but next year will be better." Later that day, he made us pack our stuff in the motor home and we hit the road the same day. I was a worried about where we would end up but at the same time I just prayed it would be better than where we were.

On the other hand, the small town gang that I was affiliated with, I couldn't let them find out I was leaving, otherwise they would have beat me again or probably would've tried to kill me. My sister and I said our goodbyes to her friend, Ash, and her mom before we hit the road. It hurt to say bye to Ash since I always liked her but before we walked out she pulled me in her bedroom and we shared a long kiss for the last time. I told her I would come back for her even though I was unsure if we would see each other again.

We drove miles and miles away from East Oakland without knowing where our final destination was going to be. My sister and I hoped that wherever we end up would be better. As we drove, I looked around and saw many familiar places that resembled my first visit here. I assumed we were back in Fairfield like before. I told my sister that now things might start to get better for us. A sense of relief passed through my body as if the pain would finally be over for once.

We arrived at my Aunt, Jani house late that afternoon. She was so excited to see my sister for the first time that she nearly suffocated her with affection. My dad walked out and left us there for a while so that he can go take care of some business. My Aunt introduced us to her husband Karl, and our cousins, Al, Andy, and Cyra. I played the Play-station with, Al, and Andy, while my sister went upstairs to hang out with Cyra. They were all from Louisiana but had gotten separated from their families at a young age and had been living in California since then. They were fun to be around except when Andy would get mad at his brother, Al, for beating him at the Madden football game. I understand why because Al was a football star at his high school so he knew the game better than, Andy. I just sat and watched them argue for roughly ten minutes before being able to play again. I only wanted to play against, Andy, so I can at least have a chance to win.

When my dad came back to get us we were upset because we were enjoying the time with our new family. After we left, my dad stopped at a store where we met my big brother, Brandon. For me it was good seeing him again, but for my sister it was her first time meeting him. His California accent was so strong that you had to really pay attention to understand everything he was saying. My brother was a real laid back person who stood about six feet two inches tall, slim, and clean shaved with a buzz cut. I knew I would be able to look up to him mainly because it seemed like he attracted all the ladies and that's what I wanted. I watched every move he made so once we finished talking I can go back home and practice being like him in the mirror. Being that I was more on the chubby side, I didn't have the self-esteem or the confidence to flirt with any girl therefore I wanted to master his personality before anything else. We didn't stay long to talk with him because my dad wanted us to finish unpacking everything in our apartment.

We lived in some apartments that had my first name, which I found funny. Anyway, it was about five or ten minutes away from my aunt Janice so I knew that if we ever wanted to go back to her house we could walk. My dad rarely allowed us over there because he probably thought we wouldn't want to come back home with him.

The next day he enrolled us into a school in Suisun, which taught grades from Kindergarten up to eighth grade so my sister and I were able to finally go to school together. This school was way better than the other one I went too in East Oakland; I actually made friends that were easier to get along with, which helped me keep focused. Now that I was finally out of the gang life, it felt good to be myself for once. No more pretending, stealing, fighting, robbing, selling drugs, drinking alcohol, or facing trouble in school.

The first guy that I made instant friends with was, Kareem; I sat by him in my first class. Before the bell rang for class to start, we spent the first portion of class getting to know each other. Once I felt somewhat relaxed, I started bragging about how much of a beast I was on the basketball courts; just trying to bring up a topic that I was hoping we could have in common. I told him how I always wanted to be a part of a basketball team but wasn't sure if I could since my dad was strict about everything we wanted to do. On top of that, I never played an organized sport; I just played street ball growing up. Come to find out he was the point guard and team captain. That made me want to take back all the bragging I was doing on myself! He challenged me to a one on one game against him when recess rolled around.

When the bell rang again, my heart dropped because I didn't know exactly if I would be prepared to play a game against him, and I wanted to win so bragging rights would be in my favor. People started surrounding the court where we were getting ready to play as if a real basketball game was about to take place. The game started off good; every time he scored I scored keeping the game even until about halfway through when I started getting tired. Tied at six, he slowly started pulling away getting closer to the final score of twelve. I scored a couple more points, but he kept driving the ball to the goal making it hard for me to cover him because I was about three inches shorter than him. Even though I didn't win, I earned my stripes just by stepping on the court because nobody ever wanted to challenge him.

That night when I went home I asked my dad if I could join the basketball team and surprisingly he let me. When the first tryouts came around, I wanted to show my eagerness to play so I showed up an hour early. Since earning the respect from the team captain I landed the starting shooting guard position playing right on side of him. The coach began designing plays just for me when he noticed my ability to shoot threes. My favorite spot on the court was the left corner three-pointer; I was always too scared to drive the ball to the goal because I knew I was never going to make it being that I was shorter than everyone else.

Our team was doing well all year until we played a school that was known for being racist towards teams that had blacks. We had mostly African Americans, so people would taunt at us as we walked into the gym, throw stuff at us from the stands as if no rules applied when it came to this big rival game. Despite all the taunting from the fans, we managed to keep the game close up until the fourth quarter. As the game winded down and the heat turned up I pulled a LeBron James move and took my headband off showing that I was about to elevate my game to the next level. With about two minutes left, we were down by four points until one of our players made a three bringing us within a one point deficit. We tighten up on defense running a full court trap, hoping that we could stop them and force a turn over. When they threw the ball in, one of our players tipped it and stole it with roughly thirty seconds left. My teammate threw me the ball but after a few dribbles I tossed it to Kareem who was guarded by two people and still managed to make a three pointer allowing us to win the game. After the game, while everybody celebrated with their families I looked around the stands hoping my dad would be there but he never showed up to any of my games.

When he came pick me up, the only thing on his mind was the leather jacket that I lost earlier that day which he claimed to be expensive. He yelled at me the whole ride home swinging on me in the backseat hitting me in the face until blood leaked heavily from my nose. When we got back to the apartment, I ran to the bathroom crying trying to keep my head tilted up so the bleeding can stop. With no care in the world, he just went to the living room and began watching TV like nothing happened. My sister saw me cleaning my face and ran in the bathroom behind me to help. She cried just by seeing me cry and when my dad heard us both crying he sent us to our separate rooms forcing us to go to bed.

Around ten O' clock that night; I was walking to the kitchen to get something to drink and saw him with a band around his arm as if he were preparing to put a needle through it but I wasn't sure. I came to a complete stop backing up halfway in the hallway trying to peek and see what he was actually doing. When he heard my footsteps, he looked back and caught me peeping and started yelling, "get out of here! Go back to your damn room." I couldn't sleep thinking he would come back in my room to beat me. I said a prayer,

> "Dear God if you really exist allow me and my sister a way out of this hell hole. I pray that one day we can return back home to our actual family so that we can be safe again. Lord I know my faith in you is not as strong as you would like but you know that I am trying to believe that you will keep us protected at all cost. I still question you at times because I want to know the answers for all the suffering we are living through right now.

I don't understand what is going on at all. Help me please. In Jesus name. Amen"

For some reason I still couldn't sleep and it was already one O' clock in the morning at this time. I don't know what got into me but I walked back to the kitchen and saw him lying down on his back with his fingers intertwined over his stomach as if he were lying in a casket. I snuck into the kitchen grabbing the biggest knife I could find. It felt as if I had no control over the situation but I can remember what happened very vividly. Evil thoughts crossed my mind, as I stepped over his resting body pointing the knife directly over his heart preparing to stab him dead. My body began trembling with a cold sweat to follow. My thoughts were scrambling like a game of dominoes. Voices began popping up in my head that had me standing there confused not knowing what to do. One voice told me to do it and everything will get better but another voice told me to stop because it could ruin my life. Shaking, trembling, what to do? What to do? Then I stopped and what made me stop is the thought of my sister being left alone, and me never getting to heaven so that I can have another chance to see my mom since I would probably go to hell for what I did. Eventually, I put the knife back in the drawer where I found it then forced myself to sleep.

Not too long later, the sun came up; thankfully it was the weekend so I didn't have to get up early. I walked in the living room but my dad was already gone. My sister and I went in the kitchen looking for something to eat in a nearly empty refrigerator. The only groceries that were in it were eggs, milk, water, and maybe a few pieces of ham. On top of the refrigerator we had cereal but every spoon had a burn mark on the bottom of it from him using it to cook his drugs with. Every morning we had to deal with not having a normal breakfast. Without anything to eat, we just sat around waiting for him to get home hoping he would bring some food along with him.

My sister was on our desktop computer playing on MySpace, while I sat in the living room watching TV. It was almost twelve-noon and we still haven't heard anything from him yet, but as I reached for the phone to call him, I heard him coming up the stairs. Accompanying him was his good friend Doug, who I called the short version of T-Pain because he looked like him just without the dreads. My dad brought us some McDonald's and told us to go eat in the room so he and Doug could talk.

A few hours later, I heard a woman come into our apartment, but she only stayed for a brief moment. Being the nosy kid I was, I stood by my room door listening to what was going on. The door opened and closed again but it seemed as if someone had left. I went back to eating my McDonald's before my fries got cold because that was the best part. About ten minutes later there was another knock on the door. In the middle of a bite, I got up and headed towards my room door being nosy again. When my dad asked who it was I could slightly hear a woman's voice so I figured she was back. Not thinking much of it, I started walking to the living room pretending to want some water so I could see what was going on. As I was about to turn into the kitchen, a big black man kicked the front door in along with another following behind him waving a gun at my dad and his friend Doug demanding money and drugs. I ran to my room quickly hoping that they didn't see me. My sister ran in behind me when she saw me running into my room. I peeked from my room door still trying to be nosy but this time one of the men saw me. I can hear him yell at my dad asking who was in the back. My dad said to them in a crying manner, "THAT'S MY KIDS MAN, THEY HAVE NOTHING TO DO WITH THIS JUST PLEASE LEAVE THEM ALONE, TAKE ANYTHING YOU WANT BUT NOT MY KIDS!" That was the first time I ever heard him stand up for us like that. In the meantime, my sister and I were in my room planning an escape. We started tying sheets together but before we could finish I peeped out the window and saw the two men running through the parking lot. I can hear Doug leaving the house immediately after the robbery took place and my dad still crying out of anger.

A couple minutes later, he opened my room door fussing as if we were the cause of the robbery. All he could say was, "Fuck man they took all my shit! Y'all get in here right now I don't want to hear nothing." He pulled us both out the room slapping and punching us on every inch of our body. Watching him beat my little sister with his hands to her face made me cringe on the inside because I couldn't really do anything to stop him. I feared the thought of him beating me the same way but I knew I had to do something to make him stop. That day I stood up to him, even with my bloody face, pushing him against the wall in the bathroom saying, "I'm tired of you beating us like this! You not gone put your hands on me or my sister again and I mean that!" He grabbed me tossing me against the wall in the bathroom staring at me as if he was thinking of a way to hurt me. Then he just let me go and walked out the house slamming the door behind him. My sister and I just sat in the bathroom together crying our eyes out.

The feeling of helplessness crossed both our hearts because it seemed things would only continue to get worse. I never thought, at thirteen years old, I would be experiencing so much pain from a man I used to think very highly of. I knew that him being on drugs was disabling him from being the parent he had potential of being.

After being robbed, life for us changed dramatically as my dad attempted to keep us secluded from the world. Not one person, even our friends, could come over. Most of the time we stayed locked in our room finding any little thing to play with hoping to not go insane. During these hard times, my sister and I spent so much time together that we fought about the smallest things. Literally, everyday we found something to either argue over or fight about just from being so bored. She would run me in the closet swinging so fast the only thing I could do is try and block it without getting hit. We loved each other, but with my dad keeping us segregated from the world had us spend too much time together.

CHAPTER 3:

When the summer of 2004 came around my dad allowed us to go play outside for the first time since the robbery. I met some good friends like Jon, Chelsea, and Christo. Jon turned out to be like a brother to me that I still talk to today. They brought us over to meet their parents after we finished playing a pick up game in football. It was love at first sight when his mom Dorothy laid eyes on us. They would always want to invite us over for church and occasionally dinner. Although we made every attempt to go my dad usually stopped us from going.

We played football almost every afternoon right outside my apartment since my dad didn't want us to go out of his sight. Jon always thought he was better than me in football. It was a never-ending competition between us since the day we met. We could never be on the same team because we both wanted to be the all time quarterback. Still to this day our disagreements are about who is the best at football and any other sport he challenge me to. We will be sixty years still talking trash to each other! Even when we competed on the basketball courts, we fuss about who won more games even when I clearly beat him.

When my dad landed a job at our apartment complex doing painting and maintenance he made work with him so I gradually lost my childhood fun. He had me painting and cleaning apartments for eight to ten hour days. On days when my friends were out having fun I was being covered in paint. At thirteen years old, I wasn't expecting to have a full time job. I believed that I didn't have to work until I had got older even though I did small jobs with my grandpa when my mom was alive but it didn't compare to the work I was doing now. After we were done working I still had to wash clothes, clean the house, and be in bed early for the next day of work.

Right before school started my dad got fired from his painting job after being caught dealing drugs, but not long after he started working at a local barbershop. I was happy he got a new job because I hated painting, but I didn't like the fact he would use my head as a test dummy for his new products. I went from having Jerry

Curls, S curls, braids, and then finally dreads. Since dreads were in style at the time I kept them in my head for the longest.

Everyday after school, we visited his barbershop until he got off for the night. Since I joined the basketball team, I spent most of my time at school practicing for my games so the only days I would spend at the barber shop was on Thursdays or Fridays when practice ended early for our game the next day. At the barbershop, I spent most of my time outside practicing my basketball skills by shooting the ball through a hole that was in the roof piece. The NBA is what I had on my mind so I practiced every time the opportunity presented itself.

Just when I actually thought this new job would make a big turn around for him things between us only got worst. It was a constant battle everyday with my dad; to the point we were fussing on a regular basis about everything. The beatings were amplified; our punishments were getting worse, and anything fun to do outside or in our rooms were taken away. Our friends would come knock on the door asking if we could go play outside and my dad would say, "Y'all stay away from my house they are on punishment!" Being locked away in our rooms, the only thing we could do is peak out the window as they walked by and quietly say, "I wish we could come play."

I started praying more every night, sometimes two or three times a day, even though I really didn't believe there was a God. All the struggles my sister and I were facing made me question if God really existed and if so why is he not stopping all this madness, but for some reason praying every night to him was my only comfort. It was my only way to get through the night without the thought of wanting kill myself.

When he wasn't drunk or on drugs I can honestly say he had potential to be a great dad; I just wish he didn't allow himself to go down the wrong path. After the apartment complex found about his drug use we got evicted. My dad made stay with some old fat white man whose house smelled like dead animals and looked like a hurricane hit the inside. Looked like he weighed about five hundred pounds and always walked around naked especially when my dad wasn't around. My sister and I went days without stepping foot in the living room or his kitchen when we wanted food because we were scared that a rat or something would jump out and eat us. We didn't even take a shower; instead we stood in front the sink and washed off. Every chance we had we would sneak to my friend Jon's or our aunt's house while my dad was at work when we wanted to eat or take a shower.

Eventually, we confronted my dad about him disrespecting us by choosing to walk around naked everyday. My dad approached him one afternoon and nicely said, "I don't want you walking around this apartment naked because I don't need my little girl or my son seeing that anymore. He responded in a loud yell saying, "THIS MY FUCKING HOUSE AND I CAN WALK AROUND HOWEVER THE HELL I WANT TO." My dad yelled back, "THAT'S MY KIDS AND YOU GONE RESPECT THEM; I DON'T CARE WHAT YOU SAY." "Well you can get out my house because this is my place and I'm not changing for anybody," the man replied. While that was going on, my sister and I were sitting in the room listening hoping that their arguing wouldn't turn into a fistfight. Now if you don't leave by tonight I will have the police here to make y'all get out," the man said. My dad didn't say anything back to him; he just came in the room to tell us we need to pack our things so we could leave. After packing the car we drove around for hours that night looking for a place to stay before my dad decided to bring us by our aunt place. He allowed us to stay with them until he was able to find a place for us to live. Since Jani didn't really get along with my dad he was not allowed to stay with us.

A couple weeks later, my dad showed back up in an old beat up grey boxcar telling us that he found a place to live. It devastated us knowing we had to leave because we didn't want to go back to the beatings. We moved to another apartment in Fairfield so we had to transfer schools. I started going to a middle school, much bigger than the one I went to in Suisun. It made me worry about finding friends again as easy as I did before. My first week there was the toughest because I stuck out like a sore thumb making me an easy target. I always thought to myself is it the way I dress? Walk? Talk? I just couldn't figure it out.

During our breaks, I showcased my skills on the basketball court every time there was a pickup game. Nobody knew about me playing on the basketball team at my old school they just assumed I couldn't play good until I proved them otherwise. A guy named, Richie, would always talk a mouth full of hate when he guarded me, trying to use that as a tactic to throw me off but it never worked. He taunted me everyday until I got fed up with it and exploded with anger towards him saying, "Look man I'm tired of your smack talking, you wanna fight me cuz I ain't scared like you think." While I was jumping around getting prepared to fight, he stood there amongst his group looking around nervously until a teacher saw us and stopped us before a fight actually happened. All it took for me was to show that I wasn't going to back down from anyone and that kept me out of fights for the rest of the year.

Back at home life was steadily getting worse, only this time we were living with another woman that my dad started dating. She reminded me of the woman he dated in Oakland except ten times worst and on drugs just as he was. My sister and I would come home from school and see both of them half naked and heavily sedated, which reminded of those hardcore gang movies I watched growing up where the scene always ended that way. The aroma in the apartment smelled as if something had been dead for years and nobody wanted to remove it. On top of that, she wanted to act like she was our mother and control our every move. Even though three years had already passed since we lost our mom, we still didn't feel comfortable with another woman trying to treat us like we were her kids. I believed that there was no woman capable of replacing my mom and it made my dad hate that we never got accustomed to any woman like he wanted us too.

It would never be a peaceful night with him even though it seemed as if he was in a good mood when he got off work, but it only took about an hour for him to get the drugs running through his system. I would be in the room with my sister watching TV because we wanted to stay away from him when he started getting loud but it seemed as if he had to take whatever anger he had; out on us. For no reason at all, he would come in our room yelling at the top of his lungs saying, "ALRIGHT, SINCE MY GIRL SAID Y'ALL NOT GIVING HER THE RESPECT SHE WANTS, TURN OFF THE TV AND GO TO BED AND I DON'T WANT HEAR A PEEP OUT OF Y'ALL!" After saying that, he would immediately start walking toward the TV to turn it off as if we wouldn't move fast enough for him. He started rampaging throwing stuff all over the room grabbing my sister by the hair dragging her out of the room while beating her in the face until blood leaked out her mouth. When he finished beating her, he came back in the room beating me until I bled out the same way. I grabbed the phone and threatened to call the police if he keep beating us like this but he came snatch the phone out my hand, hitting me a few more times and saying, "You ain't calling nobody! Now give me that phone." Seeing and hearing him act like this made me cry even harder. As he walked away going towards my sister, who was also crying in the other room, he mumbled under his breath saying, "Man I got some ignorant kids." At that point, I lost all hope and just wanted to find any way possible to get out of his life. Before going to bed that night I got down on my bruised knees and prayed,

> "Lord my faith in you have reached wits end, it just seems as if nothing is going right in my life. If you really exist then why are we going through all this pain? Why do we have live with this maniac? Why can't we go back home to Louisiana so we could be with our family? Why did you give me a dad and not a FATHER? I question you because I don't

believe that you exist, but I want to believe in you because every time I kneel down to speak to you I feel calm as if everything will be ok. I don't want to live this life anymore please. If you can hear me oh Lord I ask for your protection and guidance. In Jesus name I pray, Amen"

The prolonged days with him were starting to leave us with a complacent feeling as if we were stuck in a combat zone. My aunt Jani tried to get us taken away from him especially because he was in and out of jail all throughout the year for drugs and for him constantly beating us. He would spend three to six nights in jail at a time sometimes a little longer than that. This happened so many times that he lost his job at the other barbershop because he couldn't pay for his booth. After losing that job, we moved with my cousins Ken and Jetta back in Fairfield, where things began getting a little better for us. Their mom would take care of us when my dad got sent back to jail.

Being around our cousins gave us that sense of comfort we've been trying to find for the longest time. I was hoping that he would never find a place for us to live so that we can stay away from him as long as possible. I often thought that he could be a great person but his drinking and drug addiction made it hard for him to establish a true relationship with us and our other family members. Occasionally, I would look at him during the times he would be highly sedated on drugs and think; how can I help him? Why doesn't he see the pain we are going through? Does he even care? Throughout all the pain I still hoped that there was a way that I can help him better himself.

I began questioning if there were going to ever be a way out of this hellhole that we were living in. Suicide covered my thoughts, I believed taking my own life would be the next option but looking at my sister being sad all the time is what kept me wanting to stay strong. It hurt me deeply being in a helpless position causing me to remain in a high state of stress all the time. Not having my mom for comfort during these trying times made me turn a cold shoulder to any other women except for my little sister. I didn't necessarily ignore all women but I rejected love and nurture from anyone that wasn't capable of consoling me the way my mom did.

One day, I was in deep thought like normal, when I heard a knock on the door. It snapped me out of thought immediately as I ran to the door to see, who it was as if it would be someone for me. When I realized it was my dad it made me want to go back in the silent place I was in. As I turned around, it was my dad walking in, carrying a small grocery bag. He looked towards us and told us to get our things together. While we were packing, all I can think about was…are we going back to Louisiana finally? Asking him would have probably made him mad so I just left it alone in hopes that it was what I was thinking. My dad never really said a word until we got in the truck and started driving off. The scary part was, we didn't know what was going to happen next since living with him every day became more and more unpredictable. Arriving back to one of his drug partner's house, before getting out the car, he said, "We are going back to Louisiana after I talk to some people real quick." Even though I enjoyed the time I spent with the new family, I was happy to hear that we were going back home to Louisiana. My sister and I were both jumping for joy knowing that it wasn't going to be long before we get back home.

The next day, we didn't hesitate to start packing the rest of our things. I believed that my prayers were finally getting answered even though I still was unsure if God really existed. We never knew exactly what made him want to bring us back knowing that he had a chance to lose us for good. Being that we would be going back home made us scared to say anything that would piss him off just enough to change his mind and keep us in California, so I kept my true thoughts hidden when I got upset with him.

By this time my dad got rid of his old car for a small SUV since he wanted to drive back instead of fly or take the bus. I knew it would be a long ride but as long as we made it back home eventually, I didn't mind. My sister and I were both tired of having deal with his everyday beatings and always having the feeling of living on the edge.

As we hit the road I said a small prayer in my head, because by this time my faith seemed to be stronger than what it was.

> "God, first of all I want to thank you for being there throughout the times where I really didn't have faith in you. Even though I never really understood what was going on you never let me go. You kept a hand on me and silently led me in the direction where you ultimately wanted me to be. While we are on the road I pray that you allow us a safe trip back home so that we can be with our family again. Lord all thanks goes to you. Thank you. In Jesus name I pray, Amen."

As I came out of my prayer he asked "Are y'all hungry?" We weren't really hungry at the time but I know that if we would have said no he would have gotten upset since he probably was already planning to stop. "Yea just a little," we both, said. "You either hungry or not dammit," he said. "Yea we want to eat," we quickly responded. "Alright then" he said. The whole ride, for the most part, we were silent because we both feared that he would turn around if we pissed him off.

I drifted in and out of sleep when I started getting bored watching the lines on the road as we zoomed by them. Without realizing, I finally went to sleep and immediately started dreaming very vivid dreams. Drastic memories from the bad times we spent in California kept me in a cold sweat but before I could wake up my mom would appear saying, "Everything is ok now son." Before I could open my mouth to speak to her a loud horn noise rambled my ear waking me up only to see my dad swerving back in the lane he was supposed to be in. He noticed me scared and frightened so he insisted I drive for a little while. Since it was already nighttime, he didn't have to worry about me getting caught driving without a license and since we were still on the highway all I had to do was hold the wheel straight. Traffic didn't seem to exist around the midst of the night making it a lot less stressful except for when those big eighteen-wheelers came flying by scaring the heart out my chest.

I managed to drive all the way to Arizona before my dad made me pull over to the closest rest stop. From there he took the wheel all the way into Mexico. Arriving at the Mexico border had to be one of the scariest events I ever been involved in. They were asking my dad for something but they were speaking so fast and with a Spanish accent that it was hard to really understand everything. The guards surrounded our truck as if we were terrorist. A few seconds later, the guard on my dad side lifted his rifle with a flashlight on yelling; "Get out the car right now! GET OUT!" as my dad stepped out we can hear the other guards telling each other that there are kids in the car. We were fortunate enough not to get pulled out the car; they just left two guards on each side to keep an eye on us. My sister and I looked out the back window to see what was going on and we noticed that had my dad backed up against the truck. They threw my dad against the truck and started searching him. After searching him for a couple minutes, they found that he had a passport to cross and let him go. He got back in the car shaking and sweating, with his eyes opened as wide as a frightened cat.

I didn't hear anything from my dad for a while after we left the border. I can tell he was terrified, because it was the first time something like that happened. As the long boring drive continued, I kept praying to myself hoping I can get back in the dream at the point where I was about to speak with my mom again. We had many more hours of driving left so I put music in my ears trying to force myself to sleep, thinking that the next time I opened my eyes we will be in back home.

CHAPTER 4:

A s I opened my eyes I noticed the sign on side of the road that said 'Welcome to Louisiana.' I got so excited that I rose up in my seat as if I just saw my favorite wrestler, The Rock, walking towards me. Two days later and we finally made it, I thought to myself. I tapped my sister on the leg to wake her up. Everything seemed weird at first because I really didn't remember exactly what Louisiana looked like since I was young when I left. Every time we passed by somebody walking they looked and waved, which took me by surprise because I never seen that in California. I asked my dad for our exact location and how much longer we have left; I was getting anxious. He looked over and said, "We almost there son we are in downtown Lafayette right now." I was unsure of where that was exactly so I couldn't really guess the time on how long it would take us to get home. I just sat there quiet staring out the window trying to avoid conversation at all cost.

I forgot how flat Louisiana was compared to California; it was really nothing great to look at. We made a stop in Maurice, which is probably the smallest place I ever been. It was where my dad was from so he wanted to see his brother, Rex, who had been living there his whole life. My sister and I were upset about stopping because we just wanted to be home again. When we pulled up, Rex, came out of the house wobbling all over the place smelling just like alcohol; it was so bad that it literally became unbearable, so my sister and I went to sit in the car waiting on my dad to come out. When he finally came back to the car it seemed as if he had a few to drink himself because he was talking loud towards us as if we were sitting miles away from him. We feared our lives as we hit the road again because we thought he was going to get us killed.

Finally approaching Abbeville, I knew it wouldn't be long before I would see my family again. Riding down East Street, the same street I lived on when my mom moved us into that yellow house, all I thought about was how much fun it was running up and down this road. As kids, we played outside every day until the street lights came on and I can hear my mom yelling from the porch for us to come in and eat, shower, then get ready for bed. Most of the time, we made our way inside before she could tell us anything because if she yelled more than once then she pulled out our worst enemy, the belt. Although I hated the belt, I always found myself getting a whipping because I was a very adventurous boy growing up just like everyone else. Staring at our old house, out the window of my dad's truck, I can see myself running across the front lawn getting caught in the barbwire that separated our house from the neighbors and getting whipped for cutting my leg up badly. I can see my first Pit Bull named, Ice, who was friendly to me but mean to every body else. I didn't have him for long though because he decided to break loose from his chain and eat a hole into a Dalmatian puppy that would pass through our backyard occasionally, so we had to give him back to the owner. Out of all my memories here, the most significant one I have is running all the way to my grandma house to eat her good cooking.

Pulling into my grandma's yard I can see my family already there waiting for us to arrive. We jumped out the truck and ran to them allowing them to embrace us with open arms. My brother, Nu, seemed happy but he kept pacing back and forth outside as if he were plotting something in his head. We spent a great deal of time talking to everybody about our life in California but we couldn't really say anything in detail since my dad was sitting right there. My cousin, Teedy, told them about some of the things we were going through based off what we told her when we called her but not everything. After about an hour my dad told us to get ready to leave, which shocked my sister and I because we thought that he would allow us to stay with our family again.

We didn't think he would make us leave with him again, so we immediately started crying and begging him to let us stay. My brother was talking to my dad through the driver window, as we got in the car and buckled up but I can't really remember what their conversation was about. Right when my dad put the truck in reverse my brother punched him in the face twice. My dad backed up out the driveway speeding to get away but as he whipped the truck around my sister took off her seatbelt and jumped out before he began pulling forward again. She ran into the house before he even noticed she jumped out. When he backed up to go get her, I jumped out the right rear passenger door and ran in the house as fast as I could. Since my family had already called the police, we just stayed in the house waiting for them to show up. Knowing that he was out numbered, my dad just stood outside yelling for us to come outside so we can leave.

Two minutes later there were about ten cars that pulled up in the driveway behind my dad. It was the police, along with the Child Protection Service, and other civil servants arriving to the scene. The officers explained to my family that my dad did have the right to take us back, but after the police interviewed both, my sister and I, they felt that the best thing to do is have my family file a restraining order against him. Not to long later, the police forced my dad to leave making that the last time we had to deal with him. "From this point on, he is not allowed to be within one hundred feet of us or he would be thrown in jail," a police officer said.

My Aunt went to court a week later and was granted temporary custody of us so that she could take parental rights from my dad. She fought to gain full custody of us for a long time but my dad never showed up for court. There were plenty of times my aunt tried to contact him but he ignored her calls. We didn't care if he ever came back because the sight of him made us cringe.

Our life finally started getting better even though we were still facing the pain from not having our mom around for the past three years. Everything seemed much different than it was before I left home back in 2003. The perspective of my family made me believe they lived with the every body for themselves mentality. I didn't really know whom to trust at the time because I was still struggling trying to adjust back to the country lifestyle. The adjustment took me some time mainly because the city life I lived for a while had me in a state of mind that kept me from trusting anyone even if they were my family. When I visited my mom's grave for the first time, since being back, I noticed that no one cared to even have a headstone placed on her grave. A vase with a flower is the only thing that helped me distinguish her grave from the others. Being young without a job I couldn't afford one at the time, but my next mission was to work hard so that I can be the one to decorate her grave the right way.

Back home with my aunt, not everything was peaches and cream like I thought it would be. My aunt and her husband were going through constant battles. I believed it was because of his drinking problem every time he came off sure he would spend most of his off days getting drunk. He reminded me much of my dad except he didn't beat us and wasn't on drugs. Although, they tried to make things work, the arguments always led to them separating. A few months later we moved to a trailer after they decided to give up on their relationship, which forced us to transfer from the high school in Maurice to a school in my hometown.

I didn't mind the move because I finally began re-connecting with some of my old friends from elementary. Most of my childhood friends remembered me, which was a good feeling because I wouldn't expecting them to remember anything about me. Things started off good for me, I joined the football team, got my first job working at sonic, and got my first girlfriend. The only thing I was missing of course was my mom. Being apart of the team allowed me to find the self-confidence I had lost while living in California. Although I didn't really find my true role on the team until my junior year, when I played on both sides of the ball as a running back for offense and as a linebacker and a lineman on defense because of my speed getting through the line at the snap of the ball. The only fear I had on the field was coming back from a ACL and MCL surgery that happened my sophomore year, when I got hurt running the ball during a Junior Varsity game.

I mainly started at the defensive end position and alternated at the linebacker position occasionally. My focus on the football field eventually started diminishing when I began dating this white girl that I met at a snow-cone stand I went to almost everyday after football practice. When we started talking everything fell into place and had me thinking she was my better half. I lived with the intentions of being with her forever hoping that nothing would tear us apart. For a while, everything between us was going good but the only downfall I had to face were her parents accepting me into their family. It was mainly her father that I had to convince in liking me since he didn't agree with his daughter dating a man of color. It took some time for him and her family getting to know me better but eventually they grew to love me.

My aunt didn't really accept our relationship and neither did her son, who stayed with us while his girlfriend was in jail. I believed they acted a certain way towards my girlfriend because she was white, and at the time I didn't really care what anybody thought because color didn't matter to me. My aunt and I argued every time I asked to bring my girlfriend over to hang out. After a while, I gave up asking and started sneaking her over until I got caught one night, causing me to give up trying to bring her over. Most of the time, Mandy and I stayed out all night so that we can spend time together since I still wouldn't allowed to visit her place neither.

Mandy made me feel like I was living on cloud nine with no intentions of ever coming back down. The bond we shared was something I haven't had in a long time; it felt good to have someone to call on and be there to give me that nurturing feeling that I been missing. Although, she was thicker than other girls I dated before, I cared more about who she was a person and not her outer appearance. Her personality and mindset attracted me to her the most. I fell in love with the fact that we challenged each other both mentally and emotionally, which kept me blind to any physical characteristics she possessed.

About four months into my senior year, there was a brown recluse spider in my aunt's trailer that bit me. I went rushing to the hospital, one my mom passed away in, which I hated because I constantly replayed the thoughts of my mom getting carried out completely covered with a white sheet. Since her death, I avoided going to that hospital at all cost. It was still a chance they could have saved her but gave up due to us not being able to pay; at least that's what I believed. Anyway, I went to have the doctor squeeze as much of the poison out as possible. I grabbed the bedside, held my breath, and closed my eyes while he attempted to squeeze as hard as he can. It hurt so bad that tears came rolling down my eyes After the pain ended from the squeezing, he prescribed me some muscle relaxers and penicillin to ease the pain then sent me home.

I didn't get home until almost midnight, and since I was starving from not eating for the past five hours I put some fries on the stove because there wouldn't anything else to eat. After already being heavily sedated from the medicine, I lied down on the couch and eventually dozed off watching the Martin television show. I dreamed that there were big flames coming from the kitchen. When I felt the heat burning my skin I knew it was real, so I jumped up from the couch and immediately yelled for my aunt and little cousin, CJ, to leave the trailer fast. Since she was not a heavy sleeper she heard my cries as soon as I yelled. I stayed behind in hopes to defeat the flames. The overwhelming feeling of nervousness made me forget how to properly operate a fire extinguisher even after being trained on it from work. By the time I figured out how to work to make it work the smoke had me coughing heavily, so I gave up trying and ran out of the house. Nearly five minutes later the fire department showed up and put out the flames.

I felt so embarrassed after what I did that I didn't really know what to say to my aunt about the situation. My aunt immediately found a place to live while I had to search for somewhere else to live since there was no room for me in my aunt's new house. This is when I realized how selfish some of my family truly was. I would ask my family if I could stay for a few days on the couch only to be turned around at the door. After being denied by family, I stayed with friends for a while until their parents kicked me out. I also tried to live with my older sister for a while but her boyfriend complained about me not helping out with the rent or any of the bills so she made me leave. I slept in my car for a while; I was so discouraged at this point that I wanted to quit school and just go work somewhere in hopes I can make enough money to get on my feet.

Feeling hopeless and desperate I found myself slowly getting back into the street life and rapping, thinking that would be the only way I could make a name for myself. My cousin, Jamal, had been rapping since he was young, so he took me under his wing and helped me get some songs written. The old me came back with the sagging pants, slang talking, fighting, and drinking, even though I was under age. I was running the streets at awkward times of the night stopping by any one of my friends house when I needed a place to sleep. When all else failed, my teammate, Toney, usually allowed me to stay over for a few days until his mom didn't want me there anymore.

It was hard not knowing where I would be able to lay my head at the next night. I pretended to be strong trying to hide my true emotions when I was around my friends and other people because I didn't want anyone to know what was going on. Moments when I was alone, not having anyone to talk to, I tended to recollect past events of my younger days, crying my eyes out, wondering why things were not getting better for me like I thought. Again, I questioned God asking him why isn't he helping me like I thought he would when he brought us back home from California. Although prayer seemed irrelevant to the situation I still felt the need to give it a try anyway.

> "God, if there is something I need to fix… tell me; if there is a specific road I need to take show me; if there is a mission for me to complete give me the tools to complete them. I know I'm probable not living the way you want me too but I want to change but first I need to find a reason to trust you. What happened to the faith that I had in you? What happened to you not giving up on me in my time of need? What happened to the heavenly guidance and you not leaving me alone to find out things on my own? Where are you? Talk to me Lord? When I need you you're never to be found, but I guess this is what I get for trusting in something that's not real right? Lord, I'm sorry I'm just confused, dismantled and lost, please help me find my way through this pain. In Jesus name, Amen."

Suicide? Maybe? Lose everything I worked for? Yea right, whom am I kidding; I didn't have anything to lose at the time. I thought about my football team but would it matter if I were gone? Nothing besides my little sister, kept me from wanting that thought to come to existence.

I leaned on my girlfriend for help asking if I can move in with her and her mom; it wasn't easy convincing her mom that I was a good guy so it took some time. I would clean and brush my teeth in the football locker room at school every morning. I wore the same school uniform for three days at times since I had no place to wash clothes. When my principal found out about my living and money situation he helped get me a few pairs of uniforms and tried to help me find a place to live. This went on for a couple months before my girlfriend mom agreed to let me stay with them. The only problem was not having a ride to school since she lived on the highway going towards a small town called Maurice.

My head football coach took the initiative to bring me to and from school. I was grateful for having a head coach that would go out of his way to come pick me up so I wouldn't miss school. He didn't want me to give up on school; almost every morning I would tell him he didn't have to do this for me that I could just quit and make life easier for the both of us. Negative thoughts stayed on my mind because I had already started believing that I would never amount to anything and my life has no purpose. It was a constant battle between reality and my thoughts that left me in a confused state all the time because wanting to give up seemed like the best option. Everyday, he would tell me to stop thinking that way and that I shouldn't give up on my life especially since I had made it this far. His words and kindness is what motivated me to want and finish school.

When graduation finally came, it seemed like the last four years had been a breeze even though they weren't. I had been through so much and yet my next goal was to begin college so that I could further my education. Graduating high school gave me that extra confidence that I can keep striving for more. On the night of a football banquet, my coach and the Mula family awarded me with Roddy Menard memorial award, and on the front of the award it read:

> "For facing tough obstacles with courage and overcoming difficult boundaries without any intentions on giving up on school or my football team"

Being that this was the first time I ever received an award, it left me speechless when I was told to speak about my story in front of my classmates and teachers. Walking up to the microphone, the only thought on my mind was to just be strong. Though I wanted to be strong, the tears came falling from my eyes as soon as I began talking. My body began shaking as if I were about to go into shock or have a seizure. My thoughts were scrambling as the events replayed in my head as if it were yesterday that I lost my mom. The vision of me standing next to her bed watching her body lie there unresponsive, her eyes looking like they were about to pop out of her skull, and her face seeming dry like the Sahara Desert, were all thoughts that made it almost unbearable for me talk. I can remember walking up to her bedside grabbing her hand hoping that my touch would bring her back but it didn't. I couldn't believe that this would be the last time I see her smile, hear her voice, feel her touch, taste her food, or smell her lovely smell. I never got to kiss her bye, and neither did I get to tell her I love you one more time.

> "Hi everybody, I really appreciate this award (chuckling), this is my first time getting honored for anything in my life. My mom…well…she would have been happy to see me standing where I am today (sobbing). It's hard to know she…is actually gone…and I miss her more…and more…everyd… (Crying) I can't say any more I'm sorry" I walked off the stage with my head down walking back to my seat while every body stood giving

me a standing ovation for attempting something they knew was very challenging.

Being able to go through a portion of my life without my mom and the other portion with a drug dealer for a dad, gave me that sense of triumph that anything can be made possible. My faith in God grew because I figured it had to be him that got me this far in life even though I believed it to be pure luck in the beginning. My life finally began going in the right direction.

When I started college at South Louisiana Community College, I was still living with my girlfriend but things between us started to take a turn for the worst as we began arguing a lot more forcing our love to diminish more everyday. I would seek ways to make it better but she gave up and lost hope in our future. I would constantly go to my mentor from high school for suggestions on how to fix problems in my relationship since he had been married for a long time. He offered that I look into joining the military and do something for myself because he had done it for six years and the experience he gained from it was life changing. I was unsure about it at first because I didn't want to get deployed overseas since hearing about the chances of not returning home. I spent a lot of time talking with my girlfriend and my sister about it so that I can get a clear answer on what I should do. I never consulted my family in it because I figured they wouldn't care what route I decided on taking.

In the year of 2011, my second semester of college I decided it was my time to join. On April nineteenth, I joined the Louisiana Army National Guard. I've always wanted to do something different other than living day-to-day doing the same thing but I didn't think it would be joining the Army. I was in complete fear as I held the pen signing the contract that would, in time, change my life.

Before I left for training, I tried to assure things between my girl and I were good so that I could come home to her when it was all over. We spent everyday together before I left trying to make her feel better about my decision. A week before I took I left, things turned for the worst at my going away party. The night started off good with drinks after drinks pouring into my bloodstream; I started feeling real good by the time night fell. When all my high school friends showed up I was already beyond drunk and that upset her because I became uncontrollable at that point. Later that night, I left with my friends to go ride around but I really don't remember too much of what happened after that; much less do I remember how I got home. The hangover was the most crucial part along with the arguing that went along with it, making my headache even worse than before. After we talked about it for a while, I convinced her to forgive me and not let one night ruin what we worked hard to build.

The next day, I got a call from my uncle asking if we would be interested in joining him and his fiancé for a dinner date. It was kind of random for him to ask me that since we haven't been talking much, but I agreed to go in hopes that he and his fiancé would look after her for me by giving her emotional support in my absence. We decided to eat at Chili's, a good place to eat if you not looking to blow the bank honestly. The whole night we teased the waitresses because some of them looked like they ate everybody order. Laughing with my uncle again reminded me of the time I spent with him when my mom dropped me off so he could babysit me while she went play bingo. His fiancé was very beautiful, and out of all the women I seen him with she was the best looking. When my girl and fiancé took a bathroom break, I used this time to tell him what was on my mind.

After setting my drink down watching the straw flop until the ice held it still, I said "Hey unc, you know I will be leaving for the next three months to join the Army, and I was wondering if you and your fiancé would look after my girlfriend while I'm gone?" I said. He looked at me nodding, saying, "Of course we will nephew you have nothing to worry about…trust me." Our conversation ended quickly as the girls made there way back to the table. Not to long later, the waitress brought our ticket to pay for our food.

When the day finally came for me to be shipped off to basic training I began to feel nervous as but still tried to show strength while walking away from the sergeant that was dropping me at the airport. When I arrived in Fort Benning, Georgia, the bus we were on pulled in front of a building that had a green hat standing there waiting for us to get off. For those of you that don't know, a green hat is also known as a drill sergeant. My heart pounded heavily as if it were about to burst out my chest. To my surprise he was actually calm and collective while dividing us into groups so that we can begin processing. Processing was something that had to be done to each group coming in before they could be shipped to basic training. Anxiety hit me hard as I watched other people get taken up the hill to begin there training. I tried to stay calm about the whole thing until the time came for me to go up the hill.

As we ran up the hill the only thing that was going through my mind was, what did I just get myself into? With all the Simulation grenades blowing up near my ear and the drill sergeants yelling made it seem as if I was actually in combat getting ready to take fire from an enemy. This was considered our shark attack for initiation into training. When we finally made it up the hill they made us drop our bags and lined us up in alphabetical order. I started thinking of that movie Major Payne as soon as the drill sergeant got in my face and started screaming; I chuckled a little. Even though it was unintentional, I got smoked like fifty blunts going in rotation. In the military, the term getting smoked means being physically and mentally worn out for disobeying the rules set out by the drill sergeants. The physical activities wasn't that tough for me though because I was in shape from playing four years of high school football but also because all the struggles I faced in life I didn't think there was anything worse I could face.

During my time there, our main source of communicating back home was writing letters and the only people I stayed in contact with was my mentor from high school, my cousin Mari, and my girlfriend. I mainly received letters from my girlfriend, which helped keep me focused from getting complacent. I also got a few letters from my mentor, and his lovely kids. There were still times that I would go into thinking about my mom and how I wish I could have gotten letters from her. Constant thoughts about her being gone left me depressed daily as if it were yesterday that she passed away. The friends I met there tried their best to comfort me by staying by my side when depression really sunk in at times. Throughout my depressed state I knew I had to be strong for her and finish the training because she would not like to see me start something without finishing. My girlfriend would write letters that boosted my motivation in my trying times. She started every letter off with, Hey Babe, telling me how much she miss me and can't wait to hold me again. Those words from her gave me the extra motivation to start each week with a fresh start since mail call was only on Sunday.

On the other hand, I would hear constant stories about Jody, which was the term people used referring to the person that was sleeping with your girlfriend while you were gone. That left me with questions about what was really going on back home; that thought constantly ran through my mind along with all the stress being at basic brought. I even heard one of the guys being dumped by his girlfriend because she had an orgy with four other guys and sent him a letter about it. So every time we had the chance to call home I would question her about these things and to my surprise she was with another guy as she outright told me before forcing me off the phone to be with him. From that point on, I lost all faith in something ever growing between us. Even though I was unsure what they were doing; the fact that she rushed me off the phone left me thinking that something was going on between them.

For the remainder of training, it became a challenge to stay focused because I was always wondering about what was happening back at home. I had many questions that needed to be answered and it bothered me because I couldn't get them answered right away. When it was time for us to conduct training operations in the field for a week it kept me busy enough to not think about it but the down time we had occasionally gave me constant nightmares. I knew that after the week out in the field, the time for me to return home would only be days away, and I wouldn't ready for the possible heartbreak. The last thing we had to do in order to complete infantry school and become qualified to wear the infantryman's cross rifles was run the bayonet march under adverse conditions while carrying weapons, ammo, water cans, human casualties, assault packs, and ruck sacks. This event was the most challenging out of all the things we completed throughout the whole training, and the only feeling that helped me through it was the thought of my mom not wanting me to quit. The other situations that happened in my life, as well as the current situation with my girlfriend, diminished from my mind at the time. About an hour into the march my body began feeling like my strength was going away quickly. I looked up to the sky hoping my mom would hear me when I called out to her saying, "I'm not going to give up mom, promise." Seeing all the other guys around me struggling to keep going didn't help, but instead of letting each other quit we tried our hardest to stay motivated. Reaching honor hill and receiving my cross rifles left me feeling accomplished. It marked the completion of my military training and I was officially a United States Army Infantry Combat soldier.

A couple weeks later returning home, everything seemed different; I think it was only because I had been confined for so long that it felt weird not having someone in control your daily activities. I finally had the time to investigate what was going on and find out who she was spending time with. Keeping a calm head towards the situation was my first duty because I honestly felt like killing the guy. Thinking to myself… Could these three months really make her lose focus on me and focus on someone else?

I was not looking forward to coming home from a stressful environment into another one. This type of stress had me rethinking that suicide would be the best route to take so the pain would stop. I was young and delusional and my thought process wasn't always logical. With that, the thought of not having my mom for nurture at my time of hurt made it worst. Not to long later, I got a call from my cousin in California saying that my dad passed away from heart failure. Even though I didn't really care too much about him I still hoped he would get off the drugs and make his life better. Now nineteen, with no parents and a lost path I started feeling as if nothing would ever get better.

Being heartbroken in search of anything to cope with the pain, I established a relationship with another girl that same night I went to the club. Everything seemed so perfect that I used that sense of perfection as my reason to get engaged to her after only a year of dating. Her personality led me to believe she had all the qualities I've been praying for, so I didn't feel the need to waste time. Knowing that my heart still needed more time to heal, I ignored that because I was in need of someone for love and nurture.

Since we met around the Christmas holidays, I went visit her family in Houma. I worried about meeting them at first because our relationship was still brand new and I didn't want to move to fast. Her family instantly fell in love with me, saying that I would be the one to marry their daughter in the future. Even though it was a lot of pressure, I believed that I could carry out their thoughts of us being married because I was ready to settle down and start a family anyway. The first year, we spent a great deal of time together as she would always sleep over at my apartment.

We didn't start having any problems until she considered joining the Army to help pay for school because her parent's couldn't keep carrying the burden anymore. I disagreed with her decision because I felt that it would change her life immensely and she would be a completely different person, in a negative way, when she came back home from basic training. After many arguments about the situation she still signed up for the Army in the middle of 2012, but didn't leave for basic training until August. It frustrated me to my core that she joined after I told her that I didn't agree with it. Even though I wasn't in control of her life I didn't want the Army to change her attitude like it did mine and potentially ruin us.

Before she left for basic, we tried spending as much time together as possible but with our work schedule it was a bit complicated. Arguing became a daily thing because I was still upset with the decision she made. Our happiness began to slightly fade away and I noticed she started to create more distance between us. I ignored the signs and continued to work through our problems. On the day of her departure, I held her tight, whispering in her ear and calmly telling her that I will be here when she get back knowing our situation was a little shaky.

While she was at training, I spent a lot of time with her mom and her family in an attempt to establish a stronger bond so that I'll have the opportunity to pop the ultimate question when she came home. During a function that her family had one day, I found the guts to pull her dad off to the side and ask if I can have her hand in marriage. Following the long speech about what he expects to see from me, he gave me the go ahead and immediately after that her mom and I went ring shopping. After endless hours of searching for the right ring, her mom and I decided to get her a platinum one from Zale's Jewelers, which was originally thirty six hundred dollars before the military and holiday discounts. I put a one thousand dollar down payment on with sixteen hundred dollar note left over. Although it was expensive, I didn't really care about the price because I felt that she deserved it after all her hard work.

When she came home for Christmas, I jumped for joy because I knew that she would be happy when I put that bling on her ring finger. Christmas day we spent it at her nanny house in Gray, Louisiana. After getting settled and eating a wonderful meal her nanny had prepared for us we began our guessing game. Every thirty minutes to an hour one person would go in the room to put on a white shirt with red words on it. Each shirt created a piece to the puzzle. When everybody had their shirts on it's supposed to read 'Will you marry me.' Unfortunately, it didn't take long for her to realize that we were up to something so I had to hurry up and pop the question before she made that lucky guess. I instantly dropped to my knees and before I can even get my words out I can see the tears rolling down her eyes as her family applauded with laughter and tears. In the midst of everything, a song entitled 'I found love' by Bebe and CeCe Winans played in the background. It was a song that her mom and I picked just for this special occasion. Before I can finish proposing, she pulled me in for a kiss while thanking me at the same time. It felt as if I were in a dream because I couldn't believe that I actually just got engaged. When it was time for her to leave and go back to training, I cried as I looked down to see our fingertips slowly separate from each other. I prayed that God would make time go by fast so that we could be together again.

When she returned home in March, things between us didn't seem the same as it was during Christmas. For months we argued causing us to separate multiple times. Every argument pushed us farther and farther away making me feel as if we would never find that love again. Even when we spent time together at her apartment it felt as if we were still miles apart. Most of the time I lied in her bed watching TV while she played on her computer. One day I decided to take a peek at what she was doing and noticed a bunch of different dating website notifications on her emails. I leaned over to ask her what it was about and her excuse was that she signed up for it but never actually pursued anyone using the sites. Being that I didn't believe her completely, I continued asking her more questions until she finally gave in and told me that every time we fought she used the dating sites to see if there was someone better for her. We argued for hours after she said that because I wanted to know why she wanted to move on so easy without trying to work things out.

Losing another relationship led me to think I just wasn't cut out for this type of lifestyle. I lost hope in ever finding someone that I can be with and love unconditionally. My life slowly started falling off course, as my only security blanket became alcohol and partying every weekend. I would get drunk to the point where I would smoke weed and not even know it until the next morning when the people I was with tell me what I had done that night. I hated that I was allowing myself to do something that I was against knowing my mom passed away from smoking cigarettes. It even got so bad that I almost committed suicide one night by placing a pistol inside my mouth while I was riding home. What stopped me from pulling the trigger was my cousin, whom I called in the middle of wanting to commit suicide, and he talked me through it telling me not to be like the other men in my family that took their life when stress became to much for them to handle. After hanging up the phone with him, a few minutes later I put the gun back in the box and cried heavily while driving back home. I reached a state of depression that was almost too hard to return from.

Everything that happened in my past seemed to have been catching up to me mentally because I was still trying to learn how to cope with the things I had been through so far. Drinking and driving almost every night became a habit of mine just like it was for my dad. After learning about PTSD (Post Traumatic Stress Disorder) through college and the military I began understanding why I reacted to certain situations the way I did. Little did I know that my future remained in danger the longer I held on to the past letting it haunt my daily life. When I looked in the mirror I could see the scars of my dad painted all over my body. It felt as if I was allowing my self to relive the life that ruined him.

When I got home one night, my roommate was in the living room doing homework but put it aside when he saw that I was covered in tears. He tried to ask what was wrong but I ran in the kitchen to grab a knife for a second attempt to kill myself. As I put it up to my neck he grabbed the knife away from me to stop me from trying again. The world just felt as if it was against me; my faith grew short again, the thought of my mom not being there tortured my mind, relationships weren't going good for me, and jobs became a struggle because of the stress I was partaking in my everyday life. I soon started debating if I wanted to finish school or just deploy overseas and never come back. When I got thrown in jail for about a night and a half after potentially harming someone; the little time sitting behind a cell made me realize I needed to get my life together. I knew my mom wouldn't gone be happy seeing me thrown behind bars and ruining everything I worked hard for. My former squad leader came to bail me out and in my mind I thought this would ruin my military career, but instead it actually made me realize that the leadership in my platoon cared enough to help me get back on my feet.

My platoon sergeant stayed in contact with me throughout the next couple of weeks to keep up with how I was doing and to pray with me. With his helping hand, I began reading my bible, going to church and reading daily scriptures to keep my mind focused. Eventually, I came to terms with the fact that I was never going to get my fiancé back nor will I ever be able to regain love from her family so I just let that thought go. I considered volunteering to go on a couple deployments to Afghanistan, but my leaders didn't believe I would be prepared mentally for a mission like that so I was denied the ability to deploy, along with the fact that I had high blood pressure.

I had to force myself to forget about the past, so my future can be much more clear to see. One of the things that really kept me motivated was an organization I began in December of 2012 called, Stay With A Goal or S.W.A.G. for short. I initially started right before my fiancé and I had our problems so I barely focused my time into it because I knew I couldn't motivate others if I was having a hard time keeping myself motivated. My goal with this organization was to reach people hearts around the world by sharing my story, but at the time I needed to figure my life out so I put it aside for awhile.

CHAPTER 5:

The support I received from friends and soldiers really gave me the motivation I needed to keep striving for better. Falling into the devil armpits, allowing my life to be infested with alcohol like my dad, and surrounding myself with negatively influenced people had to come to an end. In order for that to happen, I knew that it first had to start with me if there was going to be any changes taken place in my life. The thought of my mom watching down from heaven snapped me back into focus. I started becoming more adapt to the fact that my mom is never returning to my arms physically, but I knew that she still was there mentally and I couldn't let the pain hold me back from succeeding in life.

After I started getting my life together, establishing myself in school, and working to save money I thought to finally have a headstone put on her grave. When it came to saving, the hardest part was being able to manage bills and school expenses all at the same time. Feeling discouraged, I reached out to my family hoping they would want to chip in to help me but the uncle that had betrayed me before said that it was my responsibility. Not once did any of them offer to put out a helping hand knowing my situation. Even the family on my mom side told me that it was my responsibility anyway. It hurt my heart hearing them say that knowing that they were her siblings and when she passed away I was too young to even consider paying for a headstone. It had already been eleven years since she passed away and you are telling me that it should've been my responsibility! For a long time, I lost hope thinking that I would never be able to save enough money to get her a headstone.

It just so happened that a college friend of mine named, Beth, allowed me the opportunity to meet her parents. When I shared my story with her mom she felt my pain and decided to give me two hundred dollars to help me get the headstone I've been dying to get. The fact that she was not obligated to reach out a helping hand to a stranger, she did anyway and I thank God for having put me in her presence that night. I learned that sometimes it's the people you barely know that are willing to help you the most.

I couldn't believe that after eleven years of her grave being decorated with a vase of dead flowers, I was the one to actually furnish it with the proper decoration, giving her the respect she deserve. Not once did I think it would be me to do so since I believed my family would have taken care of that before I came back home. The feeling of knowing that my mom is proud of me while looking down on me from heaven gave me a huge sense of accomplishment. I promised myself from that day forth that I would continue to make her proud until the day comes that we meet again. The most interesting thing I found out about my mom some time later was that when she passed away I was twelve and she was forty-two and on my birth certificate I was born at twelve forty two midnight. I still have no idea what that mean or if it has any significance but I found it interesting.

Currently, I am a senior at the University of Louisiana at Lafayette with a major in Criminal Justice and a minor in Psychology. I am the first of my mom's five children to go to college with the intention of graduating with a Bachelor's degree and a possibility to strive for more. On the other hand, I still serve my time with Louisiana National Guard and I advocate for Hearts of Hope foundation as well as an advocate for the Free to Breathe lung cancer association. The organization I started in December of 2012 is still going strong and reaching many people around the world everyday.

The possibilities are there you just have to be willing to go out there and work hard to get them. Once I learned that things would not be handed down to me, I stood up on my feet and fought hard to make a living for myself. Not only did I want to please my mom but I also wanted to please God.

As for my little sister, she found herself having two kids, something that changed her life dramatically. Of course when it happened it left us all in shock wondering how she was going take care of them, but despite what was supposed to be a minor setback in her life, turned out to be the best thing that ever happened to her and for me because I love my two nieces. If its one thing that my sister learned from this experience, it would be to reach the minds of other young ladies around the world saying that there is no need to rush mother hood but never neglect your children as a mistake when it was you that brought them into this world.

Not to mention, she had her kids during high school and still managed to graduate. There were times when success in our life seemed so distant; it was like standing on Earth trying to reach for a planet as far out as Neptune. Those days that we spent together in California crying on each other shoulder wondering if there were ever going to be a way out became reality. The sight of our future became clearer as we hurdled many of the roadblocks set before us. Many people, especially our family, wonder how we made it through our struggles in California. After facing death a couple times, being deprived of life, suffering from beatings, and never being stable, the last thing I thought to happen was graduating high school for one and continuing to move forward in our careers. There are so many people in this world that can't say they made it out of the struggle, which hurts my heart especially because I believe that at no point in time you should accept failure.

My mom always told me, "that no matter what you do in life; make the most out of it and if you fail get back up and keep moving regardless of the dirt you still walk around with; let God handle the dirt, he will keep you clean." I live with that thought every day of my life hoping that my story can inspire others around me. Your life does not have to end when the situations deem it necessary. The unseen scars I wear with me everyday will be something that will never go away no matter how much my smile wants to explain different.

One of the hardest things I deal with now is watching other people spend time with their mom or dad on holidays and birthdays every year. On days like these I tend to shelter myself from the world in hopes that I can have my mom comfort me in spirit. I stress to the younger generation or anyone that have disconnected themselves from their mom or dad for any reason should at least attempt to fix the problem and make things right with them because you never know when there time will come. If I can go back and change the outcome of things, I would rewind to the day my mom was healthy and make sure she stayed that way; then I would attempt to keep my dad around and away from all the drugs. A good relationship with your parents is something that should be everlasting. There will be times when you hate each other because your type of relationship is NOT a friendship, so you should never treat them like they are easy to replace. Not all situations allow for both of your parents to be apart of your life, but when you do have that opportunity, take advantage of it. I still live with thought…what if…the most painful thing that could ever be painted on someone's mind…what if.

CHAPTER 6:

Poems

Here are some poems I wrote following the separation of my fiancé and I. Being with her made me realize how much I focused my attention on trying to please everyone else and not myself. Throughout our entire relationship, I made sure that anything I did involved her in some way. It wasn't until we broke up; that I realized my true happiness was writing poems, something that I should have known a long time ago. Never sacrifice your passions in life for someone else's selfishness.

Living a dead life poem

Let's see where I can start with this
How can I tie a knot, without making a twist?
I used to get mad at the world and just ball my fist
Then God said son...no...wait... look at this

Then I opened his book and began scrolling
Didn't know how to start or where to look
My head shook
So I prayed out loud to him and he said
It's okay son I'll help you prep
Open up to the book of John
And I'll walk you through it...step by step

And I'm not gone lie I was a victim to death and the sex life
I wish I could've waited
Cause after being between the thighs
It was really no surprise
But all those intense emotions
Only brought forth sinful crime

We all know sex is a moment of pleasure and
Can ruin your life
But now I realize that I want to wait
'Til I can create pleasurable moments with my wife

God knew I was walking into Death Valley
It was like living in a dark alley
I was lost and didn't even know it
Looking for something and waiting on God to show it
So I can explore it, I prayed more and he'd ignore it
Cause I wasn't ready
I tried to fix problems on my own
But God knew that on the inside I was just as soft as jelly

Just because you are alive
Doesn't mean you are living
Don't honor the worldly gifts as your own...remember
God is giving what you have so that you can praise him and
Make his glory be known

When you get money, cars, clothes
You know all those wonderful things you boast about on a daily basis
Just remember not to linger
Cause all those things that you boast about
Could be gone by a snap of a finger

Some people work two are three jobs just to make end meet
And still find their selves struggling
Trying to find more ways to start hustling
Just imagine... if you would give all that time you work those extra jobs to God
And add just a little bit of belief
He'll work for you and fill your bank account while you sleep

Stop feeling like you have to live life and do things on your own
So you don't need no woman or a man
How you know you things by yourself
God places certain people in your life
So have the gratification to accept the helping hand

Yea yea I know it's a little bit of a pride thing
But don't let that pride hold you back
From seeing what God has on that rack...of blessings
Stop stressing...and take the people in your life
Whether be good or bad as lessons

Now I don't want ya'll siting here thinking Glen is perfect
Because Glen went through his hurting
But see the thing is with me
I didn't want to give up
I just kept on working

Mockers will try they best
To devour you and just seek for your past
Don't let that stop you from keeping your foot on the gas
Just blow smoke in they face, keeping in mind
That they will always be last

No goal should be unreachable
No word should be unpreachable
Your hope should be seeable
Focus on God's plan for you
Then you will see all your dreams and desires come true

And I'll leave you with this
Let go of the past, troubled, sinful you
And attempt to live right
God blesses you through the good and the bad...why?
Because he know your true heart desires

All he asks from you
Is to pray to him at night...every night
And stop living a dead life
And like always...Stay With A Goal

Respect your parents' poem

Now this goes out to all you young ones
I want you to tune in and listen
Show respect for your parents
For them to still be in your life is a true blessing

You try so hard to impress your friends that you forget in the end
Blood is thicker than water
Know your parents gone be there for you through thick and thin

Your parents provide you with a roof over your head, food to fill your belly,
and clothes to cover your back
Now you tell me if any one of your friends can provide that

Yeah I know you try to fit in cause your friends walk around with three pairs of pants on
With all of them sagging below their belt, but that don't make them respectable
So don't try to be like everyone else, pick up your pants and have respect for yourself

The way you carry yourself in public, trust me, it leaves an everlasting impression of you
And your parents work
Do positive things, especially so you can avoid having to wear that orange jumpsuit
With a white shirt

You were born to lead and stand out, so why follow a crowd that will lead you into trouble
Thrown in jail doing double
The friends that so say had your back, laughing while you stumble
Do you really want to see your life crumble?

Go to school, get your education, get out and get a career not just a jobDon't worry about
proving it to the world, prove it to God
Most of y'all are rushing to leave the nest, without even taking the time to prep
Believing that you are ready for that next step, then before you know it
You're running out of breath

52

Be patient...take your time, your parents been there, done that
So they know the problems you are about to run into
So listen and absorb all the knowledge they share with you
Eventually it will be your time to take what you learned and get out there and grind

I know at times life can get hard, and it can make you get discouraged
But don't worry that's why we have God to carry that load
You don't have to stress no more
Let go and surrender your will, stay on the right road
And like always...Stay With A Goal

You know... I don't even remember the last words I shared with my mom
And I don't even remember the last time I seen my dad
You don't want to have to live with that
So respect your parents
But like I said before, you parents show your kids something they can respect
And they can look up to

Living in doubt poem

You ever been hurt so much
That every person that comes in your life
You doubt everything that come out of their mouth
You going in protection mode, not letting your true feelings come out

Talking about is this person real
It all seems to good to be true, so I'm gonna let this person go
Before they be another one to hurt me too

So worried that your heart will be crushed again, you begin questioning
Envisioning all the negative aspects of a person, that's why you hurting
Living your life like you're on stage, closing a curtain
Shows over before you even let it start
Now what was possible potential
You let walk out of your life before that person had the opportunity to play their part

Everyone that comes in your life serves a purpose
Whether it's a game like a circus or get serious and start working
Trust that God knows his duty
He won't give you a task if he knows you're not strong enough to go through it

It's a little thing called faith
Sometimes you have to learn the hard way
You can't treat your heart like a puppy, and cage it to make it stay
So you can avoid pain

The fear of the unknown make you want to go insane, like addiction to cocaine
Don't make everybody a victim to your painful past, we can see through you like walking glass
Just get on your knees and start praying
Please...absorb what I'm saying

Let hurt be your counselor, God be your doctor, and I guarantee you nothing
I promise you nothing will stand up to stop you cause God got you
Stop doubting everything that cross your path
Sometimes you have to get out of that car before you crash
Be a pedestrian in your life, take things step by step

Don't rush for the greatest, why?
Cause it all takes patience
Let those lessons be the reason you become tough
Yes it will be rough, but don't give everyone that cold shoulder
Like they all have something to owe you
Make a change in your life
Keep on the right road
And like always...Stay With A Goal

It's all about you poem

How can you demand something from a person?
If you always expecting the worst cause of your past hurtings

How can a man compliment you on your physical beauty?
If your inner beauty is hidden like a ruby?

How can you protect your heart?
If you don't know what you protecting it from

How can you expect love to walk in?
If you always lock the door to your heart and misplace the key

How can you say you love God and trust in his word?
But you're always questioning his actions

How can you sit in the driver's seat and take the wheel from God?
But you always end up crashing

How will you ever live in success?
If you always dreaming of failure

How will you ever accomplish your goals?
If you always halt before you finish the mission

How can you ever move forward?
If you constantly repeating what you previously committed

It's all about you
Yes it takes hard work, what doesn't?
Be the change you wish to see in this world
Keep on the right road
And like always...Stay With A Goal

Being different poem

Everybody in this world carry different characteristics
Some pessimistic, some realistic, some optimistic
Yet we are all on the same mission, praying for God's blessing
In return for a spot in heaven

But let me ask this question...
Why do women fill their face with makeup to make up a person they are not
Putting on 3 or 4 layers just to cover one spot
So that the public eyes can view her as hot
Men drooling over her dreaming they can one day get a shot

Now faced with REALity
Body starting to taste gravity, it's all a tragedy
When your beauty is no longer the masterpiece
How you gone label that?

You may not be the most beautiful person physically
But whom God made you to be with can see your beauty internally
And make you theirs eternally

You can't change God's artwork
He already painted the picture
Stop trying to change who you are just to fit in
Cause the people that really love you will be with you, time and time again

It's ok to be a lil different
Cause in the long run you will have all the ones that left you wishing
They could have stayed by your side
Now they praying for your forgiveness

Just laugh and say it's to late for that, I'm to great for that
I wish you the best but negativity is not welcome
Where I rest my head at

There will always be people out there that hate you
They be the ones that's ungrateful
But instead of stepping down to their pitiful level just keep on flight
But never forget to say thank you, they can't say you're not polite

Once you start living for yourself and God, the cost of living becomes sweet
You stop focusing on the differences you have amongst other peeps
And you smile on the daily knowing that you were made in an image that was
Carved out of NON man made concrete...

I know this world make you feel that you must reach a certain goal to be famous
Turning what was once dreams into nightmares when you sleep
That's when you fail to realize you already popular; all you have to do is believe

Be different, and let all your flaws show
There is somebody out there willing to still hold you close
And like always...Stay With A Goal

The unseen enemy poem

As I sit here in deep thought
Wondering how this pain is meant to be fought
Never thought are ever seen this day coming
I looked at you as a queen, better yet the strongest woman

Growing up through poverty wouldn't always the easiest thing
I know it was a struggle
We had many bouts like we were in a ring but at the end of the day
I can always say, "I love you"

You played both roles in parent hood I tried to figure out how you did it
Even though I was too young to understand I knew that hurt existed
But your smile...your smile reminded me of your commitment

You told me I had a dad but I didn't think knowing him would even matter
He was living in California so him being beneficial to me really wouldn't a factor
I just wanted to pay attention to you
Since you were there from day zero and every day after

I remember you in the kitchen stirring up my favorite...pecan candy mmm the best
I would come running in the kitchen, grab the spatula and start stirring
I wanted to show you I had a strong chest

Being your super hero was always on my mind
Even though your strength shined
I knew that one day you would need me to stand by your side
So I wanted to be prepared in case it came to that time

To think... I don't remember ever seeing you cry
You were working so hard to provide so that I can have the best knowing that it was taking care of by you
I just have one question... why did this unseen enemy attack you?

Every day that passes by I can't seem to put it away
So I work hard like you did with the want to fulfill that promise that I'll be successful one day
I know you hear me mom
You live in my heart now because no other woman can ever take your place

Sometimes I have random moments
Where I can feel your presence as if you were physically here
Then when I reach out for that hug it's like that feeling just disappears
I close my eyes to hold back the tears but it's clear that my hurt will never be healed

I listen daily for your voice cause I know you still correct me when I'm wrong
And I cry every time I hear your favorite song
I remember when voicemail first came out and you were into mystical music at the time
And you would end that voicemail with 'Danger' in my mind I thought it was to scare off
that certain stranger
I laughed every time I heard it

I even wondered what life would be like if you were still living
Wishing I could have saved you
Maybe I wouldn't have been the same man I am today, who knows?
But I would love to have you here with me so we can both go down this glorious road

The crazy thing is, you did every thing you were supposed to do
Not working one job but two and I'm still left with this question...
Why did this unseen enemy attack you?

I miss you more and more everyday, now I have to live with you being behind heaven's gates
I know you are safe and in a better place, it just hurts me to know that this unseen enemy
Also known as lung cancer had to take your last breath away

Being a man poem

Now y'all know that there are two different types of men in this world right?

First, there is the gentleman
The one who wants a wife, fears God, helps others, sensitive, caring, open-minded, free from any anger blasphemy, anything that the Lord cannot stand
He knows that he not perfect but he's going to work hard to be that perfect man
He is no longer in search of a girl; he is in search of woman

Then there is the player
Sneaky, always out past two in the morning
Snatching up other men's wives, making promises they can't keep
Want to be the man that lay next to you when you sleep
But quick to leave you when it's time for you to weep...Nah I don't think it's supposed to be like that

And some women or shall I say girls
Rather a man who show no attached feelings
Only arrive when it's time for pleasure
But never there to hold you during the cold weather

But let's sit and think this through ladies
Would you rather a man that forgets who you are
Never remembers your birthday
Always have excuses when you calling him to come over
But be in the bed with another woman telling her to roll over
Ladies,

Remember where you are on that man's roster
Are you gone be sitting there thinking that he know you
But he already forgot you

Stop searching for something that ain't there, leaving your feelings floating in the air
That's why I'm telling you to leave that player

I aint gone lie, front, or cover anything up
Some men done messed up the game for the dudes that's trying to do right
Good men have to try and fix things that they weren't even apart of
We have to stop spitting game because that's lines that's already been thought of

Women are starting to create pictures in their mind...thinking
That every man has the same scheme trying to get between her thighs
Players with no feelings could care less if you cry
They just there to open your legs and get the surprise
Waiting on you to close your eyes, so they can sneak out that back door
Before that sunrise

Now the question is stated...when will things change for the men that's actually worth the time?
Will women ever give us a chance to change their mind
Give us the key to their heart while we sit there next to them praying that we can get a fresh start

Any man that can keep the little things that you love the most and surprise you with it
All throughout the years that y'all are together is worth keeping
Why push him out for one reason...yea I know you thinking what if he's cheating?
I understand that... but that's when you need to evaluate yourself
Cause a man only start searching when he is lacking something at home that he can find somewhere else

What you don't do there is always a person out there who will
So check your sex appeal, I know that's not the number one priority in a relationship
But it plays an important role, especially if you don't want that man out there searching
For someone to have relations with

Now men back to you, I know I ventured off for a second
But it's time we get serious, stop robbing a women's heart selling her false dreams
Leaving her curious
If you only wanted the ass from the start
Why wait 'til things get serious cause you wanted to be selfish and now you two are breaking apart
No... I don't think it's supposed to be like that

But a man who can cook, work hard, take care of kids that ain't his, protect you from danger, keep you warm during those winter nights, cool during the summer time, take you out for a dinner and movie, maybe a lil bowling, just something fun, take you out for a night on the town cause he ain't shame to show you around, a man who will sit there and listen to your daily stories, gives you advice whenever you feel there is worries, always there when you need him and not out there searching for any new friends...

Cause in a REAL-lationship there are no new friends
That person who you are with is your ride or die
But most importantly men we must realize
That we are NOTHING, and I will say again NOTHING
Without God

Now let's be me

CHAPTER 7:

My fifteen day emotional cleanse

Day 1:

"Hatred hates happiness"

∞*Norman*

Have you ever wondered why there is so much hate in this world? Like you reach a point in life where you want to do good at something but you always facing some form of criticism for what you love to do. Truth is people will never fully support you no matter what because the moment they see you rising higher than them they will pull any card possible to knock you off your stardom stool.

Many people will find their way in your circle only to find things out about you so when the time comes they can use it against you. Those who are willing to ride with you won't look for any reasons to use you as a stepping stool to get where they need to be. Sometimes you have to delete a circle to see what's actually in front of you. It may be hard to let go of some people that you thought was worthy of having by your side, but if you have to second guess a decision every time their name is brought up in conversation then your heart telling you that it is in danger of being hurt. Listen to your heart, as it knows true intentions because your brain only thrives on instincts, which can be unreliable when trying to separate fake from real. Fake is the new real to some people, so know the people you hang out with before you get tangled up in their devilish ways.

Day 2:

"A smile can hide so much pain but
show so much strength at the same time"
∞*Norman*

There are so many people in this world that can display the most beautiful smile you have ever seen but under that lies pain that cuts them deeper than anyone can imagine. A smile can be powerful enough to turn any negative situation into a positive one but that doesn't mean that the pain will just disappear like magic. You can never truly understand someone with hidden scars because most of the time they can barely understand themselves. The strength that they are willing to show through their smile is a true testimony of God's work.

A smile shows that even through the pain, heart ache, broken roads, lost love, set backs, loneliness, depression, and anything that may have put you in a moment of failure, you can still stand strong doing things to make a better life for yourself. Let no one take away a smile that you worked your whole life to find. Your smile is golden and if anyone has the audacity to jeopardize such treasure then they should no longer be apart of your life.

Never put yourself in a, 'I lost it all and I have no reason to live,' position because that's what the enemy feed on. Accepting defeat in life is basically telling God he didn't make you strong enough to stand up and keep fighting. Take time to think about everything that you have been through and where you stand today; you may not be where you want in life but you are somewhere better than you used to be. Success is a process and it all starts with your smile.

Day 3:

"You should be so focused on your life that
you notice your flaws before anybody else does"

∞*Norman*

Who are you? That question is the hardest to answer for most people because their day is spent worrying about everybody else flaws. Some people act like they are a live broadcasting news channel that has to talk about what's wrong with everybody else, failing to realize their main flaws and what they have to do to better themselves. Talking about what other people should be doing will get you nowhere in life. Be the change you are willing to see in the world or you will just be known as the person that knows how to talk a lot. The first step to setting any kind of example is by realizing your imperfections or flaws before anyone else does. Sometimes it takes someone to tell you what you are doing wrong but for the most part you should have either already figured out the things you need to work on or at least be thinking about it.

Talking about somebody else life says what about your life? Nothing. When someone is not like you it doesn't give you the right to call them weird or different because you are nowhere near perfect yourself. If everybody was meant to be the same then it wouldn't be no reason for many professions to exist since people would be able to be self sufficient. Their differences can be the difference needed to give you that smile you have been cravingly searching for. Everybody in this world have a purpose so love people for who they are not who you want them to be.

Day 4:

"Never make your life inconvenient for
someone else's convenience"
∞Norman

There are always those people that have that 'Can I have this, Can I have that, type of attitude,' always looking for someone to lend them a helping hand but not willing to do anything to help themselves. Family can be the worst when it comes to this because they believe you are obligated to help them at anytime regardless of what you have going on in your life. When you have things to do nobody takes into account the busyness of your life they just want you to stop what you're doing to help them out.

Never make your life inconvenient for someone else's convenience because when you do so it sets back your goals and slows down your progress. I'm not saying that you shouldn't help anybody out but you should be able to limit the amount of times if it means handling your business too. Most people will take your kindness for granted the moment they know that you will do whatever they ask of you. Don't become someone else's Guinea pig because they adapted to that lazy lifestyle. It's one thing if they're willing to eventually help themselves but do put yourself in a position that will only leave you stressed out at the end of the day.

Day 5:

"Stop worrying about things you have no control over,
you will only stress yourself out"

∞Norman

Life changing events occur everyday in your life but you can't allow that to discourage what your plans for the future. Even when it comes to relationships, many people tend to try their best to protect their heart that they continue to keep distance between the people they are with just in case something happens. Living life on a 'just in case' basis will constantly have your mind creating events that never happened, which will can make you go crazy. Some things you just do not have the power to change and you have to let God deal with. We all do things that make us want to go back and change or delete it completely, but keep in mind that the past life you lived is what created you to be who you are today. Living your life in regret or doubt will not lead you to a happy lifestyle. What you create in your mind is what you display to the world. Once you realize some things are just better left in the hands of God then you will be able to move forward from those things that are holding you back. Whatever God wants for you will be there through thick and thin but whatever he needs to remove from your life will be gone for good.

∞Live, be happy, breathe easy

Day 6:

"That person who knows your past
but still wants to create a better future with you is a keeper"

∞*Norman*

This type of love is just unbreakable, desirable, and the most wanted by everyone because we all have done things that we look back on and are not proud of. The things that you experience throughout life shouldn't make you feel that you're not worth it. Let your past be the reason you want to make positive changes in your life. If you are in a relationship and are constantly seeking a person's past you will be blinding yourself to who they have become in the present or will become in the future. Stop letting someone's past disrupt your vision from the future. No one man or woman is perfect but there past shouldn't be brought to light in every dark situation. Going back to retrace steps of someone else's route will only have you in shoes that were not meant for you to wear.

"You can't erase a carved stone, but you can always carve a new one" ∞Norman

Day 7:

"You can always love the streets but
the streets will not always love you"

∞*Norman*

The streets for some people is there only form of love in most times because when they live in a unstable home it forces them to find something a bit more reliable from elsewhere. In my case, living in East Oakland at thirteen, I wanted to turn to the streets since my mom was deceased and my dad was on drugs too but I made the choice not to continue that path even though I was forced into the gang life. The street life does not have to be your only option; remember when I mentioned that you have choices, and that choice to adapt into the street life can be potentially dangerous and it shouldn't be an option. Yes, we all make mistakes but would you rather make a decision that will get you killed or thrown in jail as opposed to making a decision that can make you a role model for the next generation behind you? It may seem like a fast track to success but what you are doing is becoming the next labeled individual of society and putting your freedom at risk. Nobody can ever force you into a life that you don't want to be apart of. You are apart of it because YOU made the decision to so think about your next move.

Day 8:

"You ever lost something you wanted to find
and no matter how hard you looked it was nowhere to be found,
but when you stopped looking it just popped up; love works the same way"

∞*Norman*

Love can be defined differently in every individual eye, but most may view it as a way of having one person that will be loyal to you, trust you, care for you, honest towards you, listen to you, and be there for you in your time of need. Some people spend a great deal of time searching for that Mr. or Mrs. Right for them but they always come up empty handed as the outcome. Others may lose that significant other that they thought was the one God made for them failing to realize that there purpose was completely different from their expectations.

When you are in search of love, your heart tends to be at it's weakest point allowing you to fall in lust with anyone that can tickle the right spot in your ear. Don't allow your heart to control the bottled emotions of love; allow yourself applicable time to heal giving God your heart to repair and time that person will find you instead of you searching for them. God will never allow you to be left alone in this world even when you think you are lonely. When people leave your life God is still there sitting next to you hoping that you would accept his company. Your search should come to a stop now because you are only stressing over something that you're trying to force. Let go and let God send you what you been dreaming for.

Day 9:

"My heart is my weakness but it's not to be taken advantage of"

∞*Norman*

Keep this in mind, if you plan on playing with somebody heart like a toy taking there kindness for weakness, don't get mad when that person gets fed up and walks out of your life. There are some people that get somebody good that is willing to stand by there side one hundred percent and lose them for wanting to still play games behind there back. Loyalty these days is not easy to find so when you have someone that is willing to be loyal to you then be loyal to them.

Most of the time, I see a lot of men want to be in control, which I am not against in no means, but men you have to be able to let that women live like a free soul and her heart will have no problem being in your hands. If you seek to control every aspect of her life then you run the risk of losing grasp of her heart. Remember the heart is everybody's weakness and causes wounds that sometimes take a lifetime to fix. Men never take a woman's love for granted and woman never take a man's love for granted, you both should always seek ways to strengthen your relationship.

Day 10:

"Being lonely doesn't mean you're unwanted,
never allow your lonely heart to travel in the wrong direction.
Just be patient and let God do his work"

∞*Norman*

Loneliness is that type of emotion that can put you in a state of mind that makes you think no one loves you or even think about you the way you wish. Being lonely doesn't mean you're unwanted it just means that God is giving you this time to figure yourself out so that when it's time you will be ready for what he has to offer you. You have to be willing to work on yourself first and get to know your worth because if you don't know your worth then nobody else will. It will never be easy for you to completely love someone without you first completely loving yourself no matter how much you force love; it just won't work because your heart is not ready.

A lonely heart can create blurred vision keeping all the important factors out of sight while only focusing on all the things you would normally pick up as red flags if you were happy and content with yourself. Never allow yourself to become emotionally drunk because of your loneliness. Stay focused keeping your mind away from those devilish temptations surrounding your impulses like the veins that surround your muscles. It may be easier said than done but nobody said it would be easy that's why God created you with such a strong soul.

Day 11:

"When God calls you to serve your purpose
in life JUST DO IT, don't question it"

∞*Norman*

Many may ask well how do you know when he is calling you for your purpose? I wish I had a detailed response that was capable of answering everyone's question but that would be impossible. Your passion, work ethic, and enthusiasm toward a specific type of goal are some ways of knowing when God's purpose for you is action. When you wake up every morning with eagerness to strive for more without thinking twice about it is that moment you begin understanding his purpose. Listen to his signs without questioning him but if you feel the need to ask about the next step you need to take then drop to your knees crack open his book and seek answers through his wisdom not the people around you.

You can be great only when you believe that greatness can exist in your life. Maintaining your life should be the only thing you focus your intentions on. There is no physical award for every achievement you reach. As much as you might want to be recognized by the people around you, know that your every last goal you accomplished has already been honored by God so there is no need for a man or woman's approval.

Day 12:

"There is no better feeling than someone
who appreciates your presence"

∞*Norman*

Being with that special someone should make you feel privileged and appreciative that they are willing to spend their life with you. Don't let time force you into getting so comfortable with a person that you forget to do the little things you did to get them in the first place. Many relationships start with the honeymoon phase creating really intense emotions that are seemingly hard to avoid because everything just seems so perfect. When that phase start to wear off, you will tend to stop doing the things that made you fall for them in the first place.

A relationship should be created off of patience, understanding, communication, and space. I know we all heard of the saying, "Distance makes the heart grow fonder," well this statement is something you should thrive up on when you start a new relationship because being with someone everyday will make you lose interest in them faster than you may expect. Allow yourself just enough space to get a chance to miss that person so that when you are together again you can really APPRECIATE their presence.

Day 13:

"You can't change a person that's not made for you"

∞Norman

Making a list of what you expect from your future lover is common but don't let that list determine your actions. Creating images in your mind about what you want to see in a person will have you trying to change someone to fit a description that they are not made to fit. You can't build what's already been built and you can't humanly change someone that's already been designed by God. Who you are meant to be with will have majority of the characteristics you wish for, if not all of them. You shouldn't have to over work yourself trying to mold someone into a something God didn't intend for that person to be. Out of the billions of people in this world, there is somebody out there that is willing to love you the way you want them to love you.

When God made man and woman, he never scripted us to be perfect like Jesus so there will never be a time where you walk into the one that meet every aspect of your expectancies. You will be loved but in the way God intended on you to be loved. Sometimes you have to experience lost relationships, running into those who only met a few of the requirements you were seeking before you can have the person the fills a improved portion of your requirements. Take time to develop yourself instead of a list of requests you wish to be fulfilled by someone not capable of ever meeting those requests.

Day 14:

"Somebody who is not willing to hold you down during the roughest of times,
should not be worthy of holding you during the best of times.
Let of that sometimer and wait for God to send you that full timer"

∞Norman

Often times you might find yourself stuck in a relationship that is full of arguments, fighting, disagreements, and even torment. Your mind will tend to tell you to back off because it is not worth fighting for, while your heart is steady trying to influence you to work things out, leaving you confused as to what to do. Someone that wants to be with you will follow their heart's intuition and stick it out through the bad times. You shouldn't have to bribe a person to stay apart of your life, if they want to leave open the door for them and let them go. Don't live your life feeling that you need a person to be apart of it because you were surviving before you met them so why feel like you can't survive after they leave. Having a strong mindset is the only way to overcome a situation in which a person wants to leave you. No matter how badly you want things to workout between you two, sometimes it's for the best to let go of those who already let go of you. If they can see your worth there will be someone out there with the ability to see you coming their way from distance.

Day 15:

"Never pretend happiness in a relationship"
∞Norman

The strongest factor in determining true happiness is if you can wake up next to someone knowing that they play a role in contributing to your every day smile. Once you feel that you lost that emotion there is no need to force something especially if you have no reason to smile again. Never hold a heart hostage when you know you are not completely into that person because you are inhibiting them from the person they are actually meant to be with. Love can sometimes blind you to things you would normally realize when you are single. If you can't truly say you love someone, let it go and wait for what God has planned for you.

You can't force someone to appreciate your presence and trying to make that happen can cause a multitude of problems. Most people hold on because they are scared to see their significant other happy with another person but truth is God sometimes allow you to be with someone as a preparation tool for who you are meant to be with in the future. When God feels that it is time for you two to separate and you try forcing it to work when it's not meant to be, God will cause a situation to occur that will assure y'all separation and in due time you will realize the purpose behind it. As much as it hurts to see them walk out of your life it is all for the right reasons, you just have to place your faith in God and everything will pan out in due time.

Printed in the United States
By Bookmasters